Daily Inspiration
365 Quotes From Saints

© Wyatt North Publishing, LLC 2018

Publishing by Wyatt North Publishing, LLC. A Boutique Publishing Company.

"Wyatt North" and "A Boutique Publishing Company" are trademarks of Wyatt North Publishing, LLC.

Copyright © Wyatt North Publishing, LLC. All rights reserved, including the right to reproduce this book or portions thereof in any form whatsoever. For more information please visit http://www.WyattNorth.com.

Cover design by Wyatt North Publishing, LLC. Copyright © Wyatt North Publishing, LLC. All rights reserved.

Scripture texts in this work are taken from the *New American Bible, revised edition*© 2010, 1991, 1986, 1970 Confraternity of Christian Doctrine, Washington, D.C. and are used by permission of the copyright owner. All Rights Reserved. No part of the New American Bible may be reproduced in any form without permission in writing

Foreword 14
A 16
- St. Aelred of Rievaulx 17
- St. Agatha 18
- St. Agnes 19
- St. Albert the Great 20
- St. Aloysius Gonzaga 21
- St. Alphonsus Rodriguez 22
- St. Alphonsus Maria de Liguori 23
- St. Alphonsus Maria de Liguori 24
- St. Alphonsus Maria de Liguori 25
- St. Alphonsus Maria de Liguori 26
- St. Alphonsus Maria de Liguori 27
- St. Alphonsus Maria de Liguori 28
- St. Alphonsus Maria de Liguori 29
- St. Alphonsus Maria de Liguori 30
- St. Artold the Carthusian 31
- St. Ambrose of Milan 32
- St. Ambrose of Milan 33
- St. Ambrose of Milan 34
- St. Ambrose of Milan 35
- St. Ambrose of Milan 36
- St. Ambrose of Milan 37
- St. Ambrose of Milan 38
- St. Ambrose of Milan 39
- St. Ambrose of Milan 40
- St. Andrew 41
- St. André Bessette 42
- St. Andrew Kim T'aegon 43
- St. Anselm of Canterbury 44
- St. Anthony of Padua 46
- St. Anthony of Padua 47
- St. Anthony of Padua 48
- St. Anthony of Padua 49
- St. Anthony of Padua 50
- St. Athanasius 51

- St. Athanasius 52
- St. Athanasius 53
- St. Augustine 54
- St. Augustine 55
- St. Augustine 56
- St. Augustine 57
- St. Augustine 58
- St. Augustine 59
- St. Augustine 60
- St. Augustine 61
- St. Augustine 62
- St. Augustine 63

B 64
- St. Bede the Venerable 65
- St. Robert Bellarmine 66
- St. Benedict of Nursia 67
- St. Benedict of Nursia 68
- St. Benedict of Nursia 69
- St. Teresa Benedicta 70
- St. Benedict Joseph Labre 71
- St. Benedict Joseph Labre 72
- St. Bernadette Soubirous 73
- St. Bernadette Soubirous 74
- St. Bernadette Soubirous 75
- St. Bernadette Soubirous 76
- St. Bernard of Clairvaux 77
- St. Bernard of Clairvaux 78
- St. Bernard of Clairvaux 79
- St. Bernardine of Siena 80
- St. Birgitta of Sweden 81
- St. Bruno 82

C 83
- St. Caesarius of Arles 84
- St. Catherine of Bologna 85
- St. Catherine of Bologna 86
- St. Catherine of Bologna 87

- St. Catherine of Bologna 88
- St. Catherine of Genoa 89
- St. Catherine of Genoa 90
- St. Catherine of Sienna 91
- St. Catherine of Siena 92
- St. Catherine of Siena 93
- St. Catherine of Siena 94
- St. Catherine of Siena 95
- St. Catherine of Siena 96
- St. Charles Borromeo 97
- St. Charles Borromeo 98
- St. Charles Borromeo 99
- St. Charles Borromeo 100
- St. Charles of Sezze 101
- St. Claude de la Colombiere 102
- Pope St. Clement I 103
- Pope St. Clement I 104
- Pope St. Clement I 105
- St. Colette 106
- St. Columban 107
- St. Cristobal, just before his executioners fired 108

D 109
- St. Dominic Savio 110

E 111
- St. Edmund 112
- St. Elizabeth Ann Seton (on the death of her husband) . 113
- St. Elizabeth Ann Seton 114
- St. Elizabeth Ann Seton 115
- St. Elizabeth Ann Seton 116

F 117
- St. Faustina 118
- St. Faustina 119
- St. Faustina 120
- St. Faustina 121
- St. Faustina 122
- St. Faustina 123

- St. Faustina 124
- St. Fidelis of Sigmaringen 125
- St. Frances Xavier Cabrini 126
- St. Frances Xavier Cabrini 127
- St. Francis of Assisi 128
- St. Francis of Assisi 129
- St. Francis of Assisi 130
- St. Francis of Assisi 131
- St. Francis of Assisi 132
- St. Francis of Assisi 133
- St. Francis of Assisi 134
- St. Francis of Assisi 135
- St. Francis of Assisi 136
- St. Francis de Sales 137
- St. Francis de Sales 138
- St. Francis de Sales 139
- St. Francis de Sales 140
- St. Francis de Sales 141
- St. Francis de Sales 142
- St. Francis de Sales 143
- St. Francis de Sales 144
- St. Francis de Sales 145
- St. Francis de Sales 146
- St. Francis de Sales 147
- St. Francis de Sales 148
- St. Francis de Sales 149
- St. Francis de Sales 150

G 151
- St. Gabriel of Our Lady of Sorrows 152
- St. Gemma Galgani 153
- St. Genevieve 154
- St. Genevieve 155
- St. Gerard Majella 156
- St. Gerard Majella 157
- St. Gertrude the Great 158
- Pope St. Gregory the Great 159

- Pope St. Gregory the Great 160
- Pope St. Gregory the Great 161
- Pope St. Gregory the Great 162
- Pope St. Gregory the Great 163
- St. Gregory the Great 164

H 165
- St. Hilary of Poitiers 166

I 167
- St. Ignatius of Antioch 168
- St. Ignatius of Loyola 169
- St. Ignatius of Loyola 170
- St. Ignatius of Loyola 171
- St. Ignatius of Loyola 172
- St. Ignatius of Loyola 173
- St. Ignatius of Loyola 174
- St. Ignatius of Loyola 175
- St. Ignatius of Loyola 176
- St. Ignatius of Loyola 177
- St. Ignatius of Loyola 178
- St. Ignatius of Loyola 179
- St. Ignatius of Loyola 180
- St. Ignatius of Loyola 181
- St. Ignatius of Loyola 182
- St. Isaac Jogues 183
- St. Isidore of Seville 184
- St. Isidore of Seville 185

J 186
- St. James the Greater (James 1:5) 187
- St. Jane Frances de Chantal 188
- St. Jane Frances de Chantal 189
- St. Jean-Baptiste-Marie Vianney 190
- St. Jean-Baptiste-Marie Vianney 191
- St. Jean-Baptiste-Marie Vianney 192
- St. Jean-Baptiste-Marie Vianney 193
- St. Jean-Baptiste-Marie Vianney 194
- St. Jean-Baptiste-Marie Vianney 195

- St. Jean-Baptiste-Marie Vianney 196
- St. Jean-Baptiste-Marie Vianney 197
- St. Jean-Baptiste-Marie Vianney 198
- St. Jean-Baptiste-Marie Vianney 199
- St. Jerome 200
- St. Jerome 201
- St. Jerome 202
- St. Joan of Arc 203
- St. Joan of Arc 204
- St. Joan of Arc 205
- St. Joan of Arc 206
- St. John Baptist de la Salle 207
- St. John Bosco 208
- St. John Bosco 209
- St. John Bosco 210
- St. John Bosco 211
- St. John Bosco 212
- St. John Bosco 213
- St. John Bosco 214
- St. John Cantius 215
- St. John Climacus 216
- St. John Climacus 217
- St. John Climacus 218
- St. John of the Cross 219
- St. John of the Cross 220
- St. John of the Cross 221
- St. John of the Cross 222
- St. John of the Cross 223
- St. John of the Cross 224
- St. John of the Cross 225
- St. John Chrysostom 226
- St. John Chrysostom 227
- St. John Chrysostom 228
- St. John Chrysostom 229
- St. John Chrysostom 230
- St. John Chrysostom 231

- St. John Chrysostom ... 232
- St. John Eudes ... 233
- St. John of God ... 234
- Pope St. John Paul II ... 235
- Pope St. John Paul II ... 236
- Pope St. John Paul II ... 237
- Pope St. John Paul II ... 238
- St. Josemaria Escriva ... 239
- St. Josemaria Escriva ... 240
- St. Josemaria Escriva ... 241
- St. Joseph Cafasso ... 242
- St. Joseph of Cupertino ... 243
- St. Junipero Serra ... 244

L ... 245
- St. Lawrence Justinian ... 246
- St. Lawrence Justinian ... 247
- St. Lawrence O'Toole ... 248
- Pope St. Leo the Great ... 249
- Pope St. Leo the Great ... 250
- Pope St. Leo the Great ... 251
- St. Leonard of Port Maurice ... 252
- St. Louis de Montfort ... 253
- St. Louis De Monfort ... 254
- St. Lydwina of Schiedam ... 255

M ... 256
- St. Madeline-Sophie Barat ... 257
- St. Margaret Mary Alacoque ... 258
- St. Margaret Mary Alacoque ... 259
- St. Margaret Mary Alacoque ... 260
- St. Margaret Mary Alacoque, to a Superioress ... 261
- St. Margaret Mary Alacoque ... 262
- St. Margaret Mary Alacoque ... 263
- St. Margaret Mary Alacoque ... 264
- St. Margaret Mary Alacoque ... 265
- St. Margaret Mary Alacoque ... 266
- St. Margaret Mary Alacoque ... 267

- St. Mary Magdalene de'Pazzi 268
- St. Mary Magdalene de'Pazzi 269
- St. Mary Magdalene de'Pazzi 270
- St. Mary Magdalene de'Pazzi 271
- St. Mary Joseph Rossello 272
- St. Maximilian Kolbe 273
- St. Maximilian Kolbe 274
- St. Maximilian Kolbe 275
- St. Maximos the Confessor 276
- St. Maximos the Confessor 277
- St. Maximos the Confessor 278
- St. Maximos the Confessor 279
- St. Maximos the Confessor 280
- St. Miguel of Ecuador 281
- St. Miguel of Ecuador 282
- St. Monica 283
- St. Monica 284

N 285
- St. Nicholas of Myra 286
- St. Norbert, to the people of Antwerp 287

P 288
- St. Patrick of Ireland 289
- St. Patrick of Ireland 290
- St. Paul the Apostle to the Gentiles, or Saul of Tarsus ... 291
- St. Paul the Apostle to the Gentiles, or Saul of Tarsus ... 292
- St. Paul the Apostle to the Gentiles, or Saul of Tarsus ... 293
- St. Paul of the Cross 294
- St. Paul of the Cross 295
- St. Paul of the Cross 296
- St. Paul of the Cross 297
- St. Paul of the Cross 298
- St. Paul Miki (one of the Martyrs of Nagasaki) 299
- St. Paul Miki (one of the Martyrs of Nagasaki) 300
- St. Paula Frassinetti 301
- St. Peter of Alcantara 302
- St. Peter of Alcantara, ... 303

- St. Peter Claver 304
- St. Peter Claver 305
- St. Peter Chrysologus 306
- St. Peter Damian 307
- St. Peter Damian 308
- St. Peter Damian 309
- St. Peter Julian Eymard 310
- St. Peter Julian Eymard 311
- St. Peter Julian Eymard 312
- St. Peter Julian Eymard 313
- St. Philip Neri 314
- St. Philip Neri 315
- St. Philip Neri 316
- St. Philip Neri 317
- St. Philip Neri 318
- St. Pio 319
- St. Pio 320
- St. Pio 321
- St. Pio 322
- St. Pio 323
- Pope St. Pius V, to the cardinals 324
- Pope St. Pius X 325
- Pope St. Pius X 326
- Pope St. Pius X 327
- Pope St. Pius X 328

R 329
- St. Robert Bellarmine 330
- St. Robert Southwell 331
- St. Robert Southwell 332
- St. Rosa Kim 333
- St. Rose Philippine Duchesne 334
- St. Rose of Viterbo 335
- St. Rose of Lima 336
- St. Rose of Lima 337

S 338
- St. Scholastica 339

- St. Sebastian 340
- St. Stephen 341

T 342
- St. Teresa of Avila 343
- St. Teresa of Avila 344
- St. Teresa of Avila 345
- St. Teresa of Avila 346
- St. Teresa of Avila 347
- St. Teresa of Avila 348
- St. Teresa of Avila 349
- St. Teresa of Avila 350
- St. Teresa of Avila 351
- St. Teresa of Avila 352
- St. Teresa of Avila 353
- St. Teresa of Avila 354
- St. Teresa of Calcutta 355
- St. Teresa of Calcutta 356
- St. Teresa of Calcutta 357
- St. Therese of Lisieux 358
- St. Therese of Lisieux 359
- St. Therese of Lisieux 360
- St. Therese of Lisieux 361
- St. Therese of Lisieux 362
- St. Therese of Lisieux 363
- St. Thomas Aquinas 364
- St. Thomas Aquinas 365
- St. Thomas Aquinas 366
- St. Thomas Aquinas 367
- St. Thomas Aquinas 368
- St. Thomas Aquinas 369
- St. Thomas Aquinas 370
- St. Thomas Aquinas 371
- St. Thomas More 372
- St. Thomas More 373
- St. Thomas More 374
- St. Thomas More 375

- St. Thomas of Villanova 376
- St. Thomas of Villanova 377
- St. Thomas of Villanova 378
U 379
- St. Ursula Ledochowska 380
V 381
- St. Vincent de Paul 382
- St. Vincent de Paul 383
- St. Vincent de Paul 384
- St. Vincent de Paul 385
- St. Vincent de Paul 386
- St. Vincent de Paul 387
- St. Vincent de Paul 388
- St. Vincent de Paul 389
- St. Vincent de Paul 390
- St. Vincent de Paul 391
- St. Vincent de Paul 392
- St. Vincent de Paul 393
- St. Vincent Ferrer 394
- St. Vincent Ferrer 395
- St. Vincent Pallotti 396
- St. Vincent Pallotti 397
- St. Vincent Pallotti 398
Z 399
- St. Zita 400

Foreword

If you need inspiration let the words of God's most obedient servants light your path.

The word "saint" comes from the Latin word "sanctus," a translation of the Greek word, "hagios," which means "holy." While all of us are capable of holiness, canonization is the Church's official recognition that a particular person displayed an extraordinary degree of holiness, or devotion to God, during his or her time on Earth. There is much to be learned from the words, acts, and lives of the saints of the Roman Catholic Church. They provide undeniable examples of the best that humankind is capable of—virtues like kindness, charity, love for each other, especially for the lowest and the least among us, courage in the face of adversity, humility, and selflessness. They embody the deepest love a person can have for God through their willingness to sacrifice all, even their lives, for their faith. They remind us that in our darkest moments we are not alone, and in our joys and triumphs they are reminders of God's grace.

You can take a few minutes every day to read one of the 365 quotes in this book and the accompanying text. Some start each day with prayer and devotional reading, and they carry that bit of serenity with them throughout their day. Others prefer to save these readings until the day is done, drifting to sleep wrapped in the warm blanket of God's love. We hope that the wisdom of the ages, as articulated through the words of the saints, find their way into your heart.

"Charity may be a very short word, but with its tremendous meaning of pure love, it sums up man's entire relation to God and to his neighbor."
– **St. Aelred of Rievaulx**

Born into a family of married Saxon priests in 1110, Aelred's intellect and talents as a writer were recognized from an early age. He was a kind and compassionate man, and the membership of the Cistercian community at Rievaulx grew dramatically under his leadership. The era in which Aelred lived was known as the Age of Friendship, a time when troubadours traveled the land singing of courtly love. Aelred focused on the spiritual aspects of love and wrote extensively about friendship as an earthly representation of the relationship between God and humankind. In a series of imaginary conversations between Aelred and three other monks, he described spiritual friendship as a sacrament through which we experience God's love. By sharing and listening, giving and receiving, Aelred believed that we participate in a relationship that emulates the interaction among the three persons of the Trinity. In fact, he stated that there are three persons involved in a Christian friendship, the third being Christ.

> "Jesus Christ, Lord of all things! You see my heart, you know my desires. Possess all that I am - you alone. I am your sheep; make me worthy to overcome the devil."
> – **St. Agatha**

The beautiful Agatha devoted her life to God as a young girl yet found herself the object of the judge Quintian's lustful desire. When she refused to marry him during the raging persecution of Decius (249-251), he publicly declared her a Christian. She continued to cling to her God and her virginity, deliberately choosing martyrdom. One of the tortures she endured was having one or both (there are conflicting accounts) breasts removed with pincers. Though St. Peter visited her in prison and healed her wounds, she was again subjected to torture and succumbed at the age of roughly 20. It is fitting that St. Agatha is the patron saint of rape victims, wet nurses, and those afflicted with breast cancer.

> "Christ has made my soul beautiful with the jewels of grace and virtue. I belong to Him Whom the Angels serve."
> **– St. Agnes**

Like St. Agatha, St. Agnes died a virgin-martyr, choosing death rather than breaking her promise to God to remain pure. Born into a wealthy Roman Christian family in 291, she was only 12 or 13 when she was martyred. The suitors she rejected, telling them that Jesus was her only husband, retaliated by telling the authorities she was a Christian. There are conflicting accounts of the exact circumstances of her persecution and martyrdom, but they all feature miraculous interventions to preserve her dignity and spare her dignity. One account relates that when she was condemned to be dragged through the streets naked, her hair instantly grew long enough to shroud her body and that the men who tried to rape her were instantaneously struck blind. Another account tells of an attempt to burn her at the stake that was thwarted when the wood failed to burn and the flames did not touch her, giving her a comparatively easy death by beheading. It is fitting that Agnes is the patron of young girls, chastity, rape survivors, and the Children of Mary.

> "Let us abandon everything to the merciful providence of God."
> – **St. Albert the Great**

The details of the early life of the man who would become known as Albertus Magnus are lost to history, but he is believed to have been born before the year 1200, most likely in Bavaria. He studied the philosophy of Aristotle at the University of Padua, but he joined the Dominican Order and switched to the study of theology after an encounter with the Blessed Virgin Mary in his mid-twenties. A renowned scholar and lecturer, he became the first German Dominican to become a Master of Theology and went on to become the chair of theology at the College of St. James and the teacher of Thomas Aquinas. After an illustrious academic career, Albert served for three years as bishop of Regensburg but resigned because he felt ill-suited to the life of a bishop. He spent the last six years of his life defending the works of Thomas Aquinas, who predeceased him. Albertus Magnus is best known for his prolific writings on a wide variety of subjects, particularly in the sciences. He died in 1280, was beatified in 1622, and was canonized and recognized as a Doctor of the Church in 1931 by Pope Pius XI.

"It is better to be a child of God than king of the whole world."
– **St. Aloysius Gonzaga**

The brief life of Aloysius, who was born in Castiglione, Italy in 1591, was characterized by piety, prayer, devotions, and chastity. Having nearly died in childbirth, his mother devoted both her life and that of her son to the Blessed Virgin and taught him to love God. At the age of seven he announced his intention to remain a virgin for life and devote himself to God. Aloysius was sickly as a child and spent his hours in prayer and religious studies, much to the dismay of his father, who envisioned a military career for his son. Despite his father's opposition, Aloysius taught catechism to the poor while still a boy, and while serving as a page to Prince James in the Spanish Court in Madrid, he impressed the king with his purity of soul and piety. After much deliberation and prayer, Aloysius decided that the best way for him to serve God was by entering the Jesuit Order, after hearing the voice of the Blessed Virgin encouraging him to do so. It took three years of urgent entreaties and demonstrations of his resolve (such as scourging himself until he bled) to overcome his father's opposition. Aloysius became a Jesuit at 18 and continued to serve others by working in a hospital in Milan during an outbreak of the plague. He died from the dread disease at age 23, with the name of Jesus on his lips.

"You must strive with all possible care to please God in such a manner as neither to do nor behold anything, without first consulting Him, and in everything to seek Him alone and His glory."
– St. Alphonsus Rodriguez

Until the age of 31, Alphonsus was a Spanish merchant with a wife and three children. He only entered religious life after his entire family died, leaving him alone in the world. Previous exposure to the Jesuits as a young boy led him to seek entry to the Jesuit Order, but after attempting and failing to meet the educational requirements, he was finally admitted as a lay brother at age 40. For 46 years he served in the humble position of porter, or doorkeeper, at the Jesuit College at Majorca. He spoke of regarding every ring of the bell as possibly announcing a visit by God. Alphonsus was 54 when he made his final vows. Highly regarded by his superiors for his piety and his good works in the community, he was often invited to preach on feast days. He died at the age of 85, was declared Venerable nine years later, and was named a special patron of Majorca in 1633. The expulsion of the Jesuit Order from Spain delayed his beatification until 1825, and he was canonized in 1887.

"Oh! happy is he who can say, 'I have despised the kingdom of the world, and all the glory of the time, for the love of my Lord Jesus Christ.'"
– **St. Alphonsus Maria de Liguori**

Alphonsus Maria de Liguori, born near Naples, Italy in 1696, prepared for a life in the secular world by earning his doctorate from the University of Naples at age 16, and began practicing law at 19. He experienced great success, but having been raised in a pious home by devout parents, he did not lose touch with his faith. A crushing legal defeat due to a mistake he made while representing Duke Orsini led him to believe that God had caused his humiliation to call him to the priesthood. His family opposed his decision, so he agreed that although he would become a priest, he would live at home and serve as a secular missionary. After six years of mission work throughout Naples, he founded the Congregation of the Most Holy Redeemer, but within a year, all but one lay brother had left. Undefeated, Alphonsus started over again, forming a new congregation for men and another for women. He enjoyed his missions in the countryside surrounding Naples and turned down the opportunity to serve as bishop of Palermo, but in 1762 felt he had no choice but to obey the Pope's command to become bishop of St. Agatha of the Goths.

"They are different from the rich in earthly desires, who, in the present life, whatever riches they possess, are always poor, and live discontented; for the good things of this life do not satisfy our thirst, however much they are increased; wherefore, these persons are never contented, never attaining to the acquisition of what they desire."
– St. Alphonsus Maria de Liguori

In 1762, while Alphonsus Maria de Liguori was serving as bishop of St. Agatha of the Goths outside of Naples, Pope Clement XIV lay dying in Rome, 200 kilometers away, his mind uneasy over having succumbed to the pressure to suppress the Jesuit order. Eyewitnesses reported the arrival of Alphonsus to comfort him in his final moments. But at the very same time, Alphonsus was known to be in his diocese. Thus, Alphonsus performed the miracle of bilocation, being present in two places at the same time.

"Our prayers are so dear to God, that he has appointed the angels to present them to him as soon as they come forth from our mouths."
– **St. Alphonsus Maria de Liguori**

Alphonsus Maria de Liguori strongly believed that daily prayer was essential to loving God and coming to know Him. He regarded *The Great Means of Prayer* as his most important book because it explains that humans cannot resist evil and observe all the commandments except through the grace of God. Following the teachings of St. Augustine, Alphonsus wrote that God gives His graces only to those who ask for them, that "God does not refuse anyone the grace of prayer," and that salvation can be found only through prayer.

"Between the sufferings of the soul and those of the body there is no comparison."
– **St. Alphonsus Maria de Liguori**

Alphonsus Maria de Liguori was no stranger to physical suffering. Struck by a rheumatic illness in 1768 while serving as Bishop of St. Agatha of the Goths, he suffered great pain for the remaining 19 years of his life. The vertebrae in his neck collapsed until his head was pressing on his neck with enough force to hinder his breathing, but rather than complaining, he thanked God for allowing him to suffer and experience something of what Jesus endured on the Cross. He asked only to be spared in eternity. Due to his illness, Bishop de Liguori resigned in 1775 to spend his remaining years writing. At his death in 1787, his last words were "My Jesus, my Jesus, do not leave me!"

"When we have to reply to someone who speaks harshly to us, we must always do it with gentleness. If we are angry, it is better to keep silence."
– **St. Alphonsus Maria de Liguori**

Alphonsus Maria de Liguori urged all who would listen and who read his words not to wait until the moment of death to seek salvation. He explained that it was only prudent to settle the affairs of one's conscience while the opportunity exists, as death can come with no warning. Alphonsus encouraged the rural missionaries to spend much time listening to confessions and comforting the penitent with patience and compassion, explaining that "The more deeply a soul is mired in evil, the more necessary it is to receive him well, in order to extract him from the claws of the enemy."

> "He who desires nothing but God is rich and happy."
> – **St. Alphonsus Maria de Liguori**

Young Alphonsus was educated at home by tutors under his father's watchful eye. He played the harpsichord masterfully by the time he was 13, enjoyed riding and fencing, and played cards in the evenings. He loved the opera but found theatres morally suspect. He could easily have been seduced by frivolous pleasures and the attention he received during his years as a successful lawyer, and he admitted to spending more time in society and praying less than he should have, but he remained modest and pure. When asked later in life whether Alphonsus had shown any humor in his youth, a childhood friend answered, "Never!" Alphonsus later wrote, "Banquets, entertainments, theatres, these are the pleasures of the world, but pleasures which are filled with the bitterness of gall and sharp thorns. Believe me who have experienced it, and now weep over it."

"A single bad book will be sufficient to cause the destruction of an entire monastery."
– **St. Alphonsus Maria de Liguori**

When Alphonsus accepted the see of St. Agatha of the Goths, he found a community of more than 30,000 people and 400 priests. The people were woefully ignorant about God and the Church, and the priests weren't doing much to change that situation. Through his preaching and leadership, Alphonsus brought about a dramatic change in the city. He insisted on the proper observance of religious rites and imposed more rigorous standards for acceptance into the priesthood. Within a relatively short period of time, the people began participating in Communion and Confession, attending services, and growing closer to God.

> "As a mother delights in taking her child on her knees, in caressing and feeding him, so does our God delight in treating with love and tenderness those souls who give themselves entirely to Him and place all their hopes in His goodness and bounty."
> **– St. Alphonsus Maria de Liguori**

In a time when many thought of God as strict and merciless, Alphonsus Maria de Liguori emphasized the goodness and loving heart of Jesus, but in conjunction with the concept of God's infinite justice. He reminded the people that "Mercy is promised to those who fear God and not to those who abuse His mercy." His writings about morality and theology contributed to Alphonsus, beatified in 1816 and canonized in 1839, being declared a Doctor of the Church in 1871 by Pope Pius IX.

"Grow in virtue, in order that the sanctity of this House may last forever, passing on its good traditions to those who come after you. Love one another that charity may be the bond at all times uniting you to all in Jesus Christ."
– **St. Artold the Carthusian**

Artold was a member of the contemplative Carthusian order that traces its roots to the French Alps in 1084 and now has 450 monks and nuns living on three continents. Carthusian monks of St. Artold's time lived solitary lives. Unlike other cloistered orders that lived, ate, worked, and worshipped together, Carthusians rarely left their cells. They lived in silence and solitude except when sharing the liturgy, and this tradition continues today. St. Artold was known for his piety and was the founder and first Prior of the Charterhouse of Arvières in the diocese of Geneva. When chosen to serve as Bishop of Belley, the prospect terrified him, and he hid himself away, but he was found and reluctantly accepted the position. Miracles after his death at the reported age of 105 led to his canonization.

> "When we find ourselves in some danger, we must not lose courage, but confide much in the Lord; for where danger is great, great also is the assistance of Him who is called our Helper in tribulation."
> **– St. Ambrose of Milan**

Ambrose was no stranger to danger. As bishop of Milan, Ambrose faced opposition from the imperial family, which backed the Arians. The Arians did not view Christ as fully divine and were considered heretics by the ecclesiastical authorities. Emperor Valentinian II was a young child when he ascended the imperial throne, and his mother Justina, who wielded the real power during his reign, was an Arian. Ambrose's refusal to accede to their demand that the Arians be given the use of one of Milan's three basilicas led him and his supporters to barricade themselves inside the basilica. Despite the obvious risks of challenging Valentinian and Justina, Ambrose maintained that "The emperor is in the church, not above it," and they backed down.

"The rich man who gives to the poor does not bestow alms but pays a debt."
– **St. Ambrose of Milan**

Born to Roman Christian parents in the part of Gaul that is now Germany, Ambrose studied law, literature, and rhetoric in Rome and became consular prefect, or governor, of Liguria and Emilia at the age of 32, with headquarters in Milan. He became bishop of Milan two years later by popular acclamation though he was not even a priest. He gave away his property, studied theology, and became such a strong defender of the Catholic faith that he was named a Doctor of the Church. He was particularly known for the hymns he wrote to spread the gospel. His compassion for the poor and his own rejection of material wealth led to his being known as the patron saint of beggars.

> "If it is 'daily bread,' why do you take it once a year? ... Take daily what is to profit you daily. Live in such a way that you may deserve to receive it daily. He who does not deserve to receive it daily, does not deserve to receive it once a year."
> – **St. Ambrose of Milan**

You've probably heard the saying, "When in Rome, do as the Romans do." But you may not be aware that it has its origins in Ambrose's advice to Augustine of Hippo to observe the religious customs of the Church wherever he might be at the time. He told Augustine that when he was in Rome, he fasted on Saturday, as that was the local custom. However, when he was in Milan, where fasting on Saturday was not the custom, Ambrose did not fast either. "Follow the custom of the church where you are," he suggested to Augustine. Ambrose was known for his flexibility in the manner of public worship. He viewed the liturgy as a tool for the use of the people in worshipping God, and therefore liturgy was adaptable to reflect local custom.

"I stand between two eternities. I must fall either into one or the other."
– **St. Ambrose of Milan**

St. Ambrose is credited with several miraculous healings. For example, while he was staying in Rome in the year 382, a woman who was bedridden with palsy was carried to where Ambrose was saying mass, and she begged him to intercede with God on her behalf. According to the account of Paulinus, the ailing woman kissed the hem of Ambrose's garments while he was praying and laying hands on her, and she instantly regained the ability to walk. He is also said to have driven a demon from a possessed person by touching him with linen used to soak up the blood of the martyrs Nazarius and Celus, whose bodies Ambrose had discovered in a garden near Milan.

"Our own evil inclinations are far more dangerous than any external enemies."
– **St. Ambrose of Milan**

Ambrose was fearless in his defense of the Faith and espousing the gospel. Even the emperor was not immune to Ambrose's chastisement for wrongdoing. When the emperor ordered the execution of 7,000 people in retribution for the murder of a Roman governor, Ambrose excommunicated the emperor and required him to do penance in public for not following the gospel and causing the deaths of so many innocents for the sin of one man.

> "No one heals himself by wounding another."
> – **St. Ambrose of Milan**

There's an interesting reason for St. Ambrose being the patron saint of beekeepers. The story is that a swarm of bees landed on the face of the infant Ambrose, leaving behind a drop of honey when they flew away. Ambrose was not harmed, and his father saw the single drop of honey as a sign that his son would grow up to be a gifted speaker, which was, in fact, the case. Whether entirely a natural gift or the result of studying rhetoric and law, Ambrose was known to speak and write eloquently with the goal of spreading the gospel.

> "The Lord was baptized, not to be cleansed Himself, but to cleanse the waters, so that those waters, cleansed by the flesh of Christ which knew no sin, might have the power of baptism."
> – **St. Ambrose of Milan**

In the year 374, Ambrose enjoyed great popularity as Governor of Aemilia-Liguria in northern Italy. Amid great controversy over the selection of a successor to the Bishop of Milan after his death, Ambrose traveled to the church where the election was to be held, hoping to prevent a crisis. As he addressed the assemblage, a great cry went up for Ambrose himself to become bishop, though he had never been baptized or formally trained in theology. Considering himself unqualified, Ambrose fled the crowd and hid away in a friend's home. But when a letter applauding the choice of Ambrose was received from the Emperor, Ambrose's friend refused to conceal him, and within a week, Ambrose was baptized, ordained, and consecrated as bishop of Milan.

> "By Christ's Passion our weakness was cured. By His Resurrection death was conquered. Still we have to be sorrowful for the world, as well as joyful in the Lord, sorrowful in penance, joyful in gratitude."
> **– St. Ambrose of Milan**

Ambrose is said to have resurrected an infant while staying in the home of Decentius, a prominent citizen or Florence. While Ambrose was away on a trip, the infant son of Decentius died, and the mother laid him upon Ambrose's bed. When Ambrose returned from his trip, he laid upon the child's body, emulating the actions by which Elisha resurrected the son of a rich woman of Sunam in gratitude for her hospitality. Through his prayers, Ambrose restored life to the son of Decentius.

"When we find ourselves in some grave danger, we must not lose courage but firmly trust in God, for where there is the greatest danger, there is also the greatest help from Him who wants to be called our 'Help' in times of peace and in times of tribulation."
– St. Ambrose of Milan

Ambrose of Milan died in Rome on the eve of Easter in the year 397. His death was accompanied by several miracles, including his appearance in a vision to a group of children who were being baptized that night. He was interred beneath the altar in the Ambrosian basilica in Milan, between the bodies of St. Gervase and St. Protase. In 1298, St. Ambrose was named a Doctor of the Church for his vigorous defense of the Church in trying times.

> "If we strive for goals, relishing in the pleasure of circumstance, nothing is enjoyable, and life becomes purposeless."
> **– St. Andrew**

The brother of Simon Peter, Andrew is known as the First Called, for having been the first of the Apostles to follow Jesus. While Peter was a gifted and persuasive speaker, Andrew was regarded as practical and apparently played an administrative role among the disciples of Jesus. His practical nature is seen in the account of the multiplication of the loaves and fish in Galilee. It was Andrew who called Jesus' attention to the young boy who had the five loaves and two fish. It was also Andrew who pointed out the inadequacy of that small amount of food to satisfy the multitudes. Like Jesus, Andrew died on the cross, but it took him two days to succumb. According to the sixth century story of the Passion of Andrew, the Apostle came to the cross full of joy and confidence: "O blessed Cross, clothed in the majesty and beauty of the Lord's limbs!... Take me, carry me far from men, and restore me to my Teacher, so that, through You, the One who redeemed me by You, may receive me. Hail, O Cross; yes, hail indeed!"

> "It is with the smallest brushes that the artist paints the most exquisitely beautiful pictures."
> **– St. André Bessette**

Alfred Bessette (1845-1937) was a sickly child, who grew into a sickly young man, and was fired from one job after another for not being strong enough to do much work. Though he was accepted into the novitiate of the Holy Cross Brothers, he once again was asked to leave, but a visiting bishop was impressed with his devotion to God and Saint Joseph and allowed him to stay. He took the name Brother Andre and worked as the doorkeeper at Notre Dame College in Montreal for forty years. His greatest desire was to build a mountaintop chapel dedicated to Saint Joseph, but the Archbishop told him he could build one only if he could pay for it. After years of collecting nickels and dimes and quarters, he had a few hundred dollars saved and began building, a little at a time, as he collected more donations, many of them from people who experienced healing on the mountaintop. His deep devotion to St. Joseph was his motivation to keep persevering. When the chapel was done, he started to build a basilica, but he didn't live to see it finished. The sickly man who was considered too weak to do any work of value lived to the age of 92, never wavering in his devotion. He was canonized in 2010 by Pope Benedict XVI.

"I urge you to remain steadfast in faith, so that at last we will all reach heaven and there rejoice together."
– **St. Andrew Kim Taegon**

Andrew Kim Taegon was the first Korean-born priest and pastor and became the patron saint of Korea. The son of Korean Christian converts, he attended seminary in Macao, China and was ordained in Shanghai. After its introduction into Korea by Japanese Christian soldiers during the Japanese invasion of 1592, Christianity flourished under lay leadership during the 17th century, even while Korea was a closed society. However, the 19th century saw three terrible waves of persecution in 1839, 1866, and 1867. A total of 103 Korean Christians, mostly lay people, were tortured and martyred, Andrew's father among them. Eight years after his father's execution, Andrew was helping smuggle missionaries into Korea in 1847 when he was arrested, tortured, and beheaded. During his visit to Korea in 1984, Pope John Paul II canonized Andrew Kim Taegon, the married lay apostle Paul Chong Hasang, 98 other Koreans, and three French missionaries persecuted and martyred between 1839 and 1867.

> "Behold thy lofty origin and bethink thee of the due of love thou owest thy Creator."
> – **St. Anselm of Canterbury**

By nature a gentle, peace-loving man and a brilliant scholar, St. Anselm came into the priesthood and rose in the Church in a time of rampant conflict. Known for his philosophical and theological writings, in 1093 at the age of 63, he reluctantly accepted his appointment as archbishop of Canterbury. As archbishop he often found himself opposing the crown as England's King William Rufus, and then his successor, King Henry I, resisted efforts to reform the Church in England. Anselm chose voluntary exile on two occasions to remove himself from the fray. He is perhaps known best for his theological treatises.

"When I am before the Blessed Sacrament, I feel such a lively faith that I can't describe it. Christ in the Eucharist is almost tangible to me...When it is time for me to leave, I have to tear myself away from His sacred presence."
– **St. Anthony of Claret**

The founder of the Missionary Sons of the Immaculate Heart of Mary, known today as the Claretions, had the gift of prophecy, and many of his prophecies are well documented. One prophecy occurred while Anthony was serving as Archbishop of Santiago in Cuba. He told those who would not heed his words that God would give them a sign, and shortly thereafter Santiago was rocked by the strongest earthquake in memory, followed by numerous aftershocks every day for weeks. Anthony told the people that the earthquakes were the sign he had told them to expect from God, and then he went on to predict that if they did not change their ways, God would strike them with cholera and pestilence. Within a short time, cholera broke out and swept through the city, killing ten percent of the population in three months.

> "Actions speak louder than words; let your words teach and your actions speak."
> – **St. Anthony of Padua**

Today, we speak of people "reinventing" themselves when they make drastic changes in their lives. Anthony's life changed directions several times, always at God's calling, though to observers it may have appeared to be a matter of chance. Born Fernando Martins in Lisbon, Portugal, he felt called to study at the Abbey of Santa Cruz in what was then the capital of Portugal, Coimbra. As a young priest, he was given responsibility for providing hospitality for the Abbey's guests which brought him into contact with the Franciscans. He soon asked permission to leave and join the new Franciscan Order, where he changed his name to Anthony. Hoping to be martyred, he went to Morocco to spread the Faith to the Moors, but he was soon sent back to Portugal to recover from a serious illness. When his ship was blown off course, Anthony ended up in Tuscany where he lived as a hermit for a while before a chance invitation to deliver a sermon without preparation led to another chapter in his life as a renowned preacher.

"The saints are like the stars. In his providence Christ conceals them in a hidden place that they may not shine before others when they might wish to do so. Yet they are always ready to exchange the quiet of contemplation for the works of mercy as soon as they perceive in their heart the invitation of Christ."
– **St. Anthony of Padua**

Anthony died in 1231 at the young age of 36 and was canonized the following year, among the quickest canonizations ever. One of the miracles attributed to Anthony, the miracle of the mule, attests to his fervent desire to convert heretics. He believed that not partaking of the spiritual nourishment of the Eucharist was as self-destructive as refusing food. A heretic told Anthony he would only believe in Christ's presence in the consecrated host if his mule would bow down to it. During the three days before the test, the man starved his mule, yet at the appointed hour, the mule chose the host offered by Anthony over the handful of grain held out by the heretic.

> "Consider every day that you are then for the first time beginning; and always act with the same fervor as on the first day you began."
> – **St. Anthony of Padua**

Many people of Anthony's time praised his talent as a speaker and his fervor in reaching out to nonbelievers. This is nowhere more apparent than in the story of the miracle of the fishes. After preaching to the heretics in Rimini for several days without changing their hearts, Anthony stood on the shore where the river met the sea and said, "Listen to the word of God, O ye fishes of the sea and the river, seeing that the faithless heretics refuse to do so." A multitude of fish of different species arranged themselves in rows before him and lifted their heads from the water to hear his words. As Anthony continued to preach, the fish bowed their heads in reverence to God, and the heretics who witnessed the sight opened their hearts to his words and embraced the faith he spoke of so eloquently.

"The birds are the saints, who fly to heaven on the wings of contemplation, who are so removed from the world that they have no business on earth. They do not labour, but by contemplation alone they already live in heaven."
– **St. Anthony of Padua**

There's a story behind St. Anthony being the patron saint of lost things. In his time, the printing press had not yet been invented, so books had to be copied laboriously by hand and were therefore of great value. A novice who left the order took with him a book of psalms that was especially valuable to Anthony because it contained notes he used while teaching. When Anthony noticed that it was missing, he prayed that someone would find and return it. The novice had a change of heart and not only returned the book but also returned to the order. Not only is St. Anthony known for restoring lost objects, but he is also known for restoring lost faith because of his success in converting heretics.

> "Earthly riches are like the reed. Its roots are sunk in the swamp, and its exterior is fair to behold; but inside it is hollow. If a man leans on such a reed, it will snap off and pierce his soul."
> **– St. Anthony of Padua**

In Anthony's time, many clergymen who preached the Gospels had no qualms about displaying their own personal wealth. The poor to whom they were preaching had trouble relating to their privileged lifestyle—a lifestyle that Anthony found antithetical to the lessons of the Gospels. Anthony believed that he could only be an effective preacher of the Gospels by living a life of gospel poverty and humility. The crowds found the example of Anthony's life as compelling and instructive as his words.

> "Thus united to them in the fellowship of life, he will both understand the things revealed to them by God and, thenceforth escaping the peril that threatens sinners in the judgment, will receive that which is laid up for the saints in the kingdom of heaven."
> **– St. Athanasius**

Athanasius was repeatedly forced into exile while serving as archbishop of Alexandria during decades of conflict between the Church and Arianism. The Arians did not believe that Jesus was fully divine, while Athanasius strongly defended the doctrine that Jesus was truly God. In exile, Athanasius lived among the religious hermits in the Egyptian desert, moving from one hermitage to another and gaining a true appreciation of monastic asceticism.

"These are fountains of salvation that they who thirst may be satisfied with the living words they contain. In these alone is proclaimed the doctrine of godliness. Let no man add to these, neither let him take out from these."
– St. Athanasius

Athanasius, born in 296 to a well-regarded Christian family in Alexandria, Egypt, was destined from an early age for a life in the Church and received an education in philosophy, theology, rhetoric, and law. When Athanasius was only a boy, Bishop Alexander of Alexandria saw him baptizing some other children and assumed they were playing. But when Alexander spoke with the boys, he was impressed by their sincerity, declared the baptisms legitimate, and decided that all of them should train as priests. Athanasius would eventually become Alexander's successor as bishop of Alexandria.

"Jesus that I know as my Redeemer cannot be less than God."
– **St. Athanasius**

Athanasius spent most of his life defending the faith against Arianism, which argued against the true divinity of Jesus. His actions earned him the names "Father of Orthodoxy," "Pillar of the Church," and "Champion of Christ's Divinity," and eventually the title of Doctor of the Church. While bishop of Alexandria, Egypt, he was exiled to northern Gaul by the Emperor Constantine, the first of five times he would be exiled for defending the doctrine of Christ's divinity. During the relatively peaceful periods in this life, Athanasius wrote theological and historical treatises that attacked Arianism from every angle. His most popular work, however, was his biographical *Life of Saint Anthony*, which promoted something very important to him—the ideals of monastic life.

> "Charity is no substitute for justice withheld."
> **– St. Augustine**

Born in 354 to a Christian mother, Monica, who would eventually be canonized herself, and a pagan father, Patricius, in Numidia, Augustine had the advantage of a Christian education. But in his teens, he fell into a profligate lifestyle and entered a 15-year relationship with a concubine who bore him a son. He was as seduced by various philosophies as he was by excessive drink, the theater, and other pleasures of city life. After 17 years of his mother's prayers for him to return to Christianity, at the age of 29 he left Africa for Italy, came under the influence of Bishop Ambrose, and embraced Christianity as the true faith. Augustine was baptized by Ambrose in 387 and was ordained in 391. As a priest he refuted the same ideas he had once espoused and had great success in fighting heresy. At 42, he became Bishop of Hippo. Continuing to write prolifically, as he had through most of his life, he vigorously defended the faith against attack by competing philosophies and theological views and played a key role in shaping Western Christianity. Augustine succumbed to illness at 76, was canonized by popular acclaim, and was recognized as a Doctor of the Church in 1298. He is recognized as the patron saint of brewers, in recognition of his understanding of those who overindulge in alcohol and other vices.

> "The love of worldly possessions is a sort of bird line, which entangles the soul, and prevents it flying to God."
> – **St. Augustine**

Augustine wrote extensively on the dangers of the desire for wealth (not wealth itself), reminding the faithful that the love of money is the root of all evil (1 Timothy 6:10). He emphasized the risk of losing one's faith and godliness, the "wealth of Christians," in pursuit of earthly riches. Having food and clothing should be enough to make a godly person content, he wrote, and famine gave the faithful the chance to grow in piety through their endurance of it and ended earthly misery for those who succumbed to it.

"Your first task is to be dissatisfied with yourself, fight sin, and transform yourself into something better. Your second task is to put up with the trials and temptations of this world that will be brought on by the change in your life and to persevere to the very end in the midst of these things."
– **St. Augustine**

St. Augustine is regarded by many as the first psychologist because of his belief that studying the workings of the human mind would help him understand the divine. He drew on his education in philosophy and theology and viewed emotional turmoil as evidence of the conflict between God and self. That conflict, Augustine believed, accounted for the turmoil in the world—a world in which human behavior is often at odds with the way we know we should act. Transforming ourselves and the world we live in, according to Augustine, requires humans to develop unconditional love.

> "There is a beauty of form, a dignity of language, a sublimity of diction which are, so to speak, spontaneous, and are the natural outcome of great thoughts, strong convictions, and glowing feelings. The Fathers [of the Church] often attain to this eloquence without intending to do so, without self-complacency and all unconsciously."
> **– St. Augustine**

It's important to remember that in St. Augustine's time, the vast majority of people were illiterate, and few had access to books. Augustine once told his congregation, "We are your books." He knew that for most people, their only way to learn and come to understand God's Word was through the words of preachers. In fact, he regarded the homilies he delivered as shared prayer. He spoke in plain language and often bemoaned his own shortcomings as a homilist, constantly trying to improve his effectiveness as a preacher and teacher.

> "God had one son on earth without sin, but never one without suffering."
> – **St. Augustine**

Augustine sought the answer to why God, all-powerful and good, required such suffering from his son as the price for humankind's salvation. An all-powerful God surely had no limits in choosing a mechanism for our salvation, he reasoned, and if He deliberately chose to cause his son such suffering, could He really be merciful and good? Augustine concluded that God could have chosen differently but instead created His plan for our salvation long before the Incarnation. Blood sacrifice as the means of atoning for sin was part of God's plan from before the Fall, and that plan was prophesied through the ages. Augustine also concluded from the Gospels that God the Son's will was perfectly aligned with God the Father's will, and that Jesus fully understood and accepted His sacrificial role in His Father's plan.

> "God judged it better to bring good out of evil than to suffer no evil to exist."
> – **St. Augustine**

From his days as a student, Augustine was preoccupied with the existence of evil. He sought the answer to what was, for him and many other theologians, a foundational question: Why does God, all-powerful and perfectly good, allow His children to suffer? He concluded initially that evil exists because God has given us free will, and it is our own decisions and actions that put us in harm's way. Later in his life, he developed a more nuanced view that what we perceive as evil may not actually be evil, because we cannot comprehend the mind of God.

> "Faith is to believe what you do not see; the reward of this faith is to see what you believe."
> **– St. Augustine**

Augustine countered the skepticism of those who would not believe in the existence of what they could not see with evidence in the form of Old Testament prophecies of Christ's incarnation, death, and resurrection. He also offered as evidence the rapid spread of Christianity and the changes it brought to people's lives and to the world around them, which he maintained could only have occurred if God were at the heart of it.

> "God has no need of your money, but the poor have. You give it to the poor, and God receives it."
> **– St. Augustine**

St. Augustine was the first to formulate a theological definition of "miraculum," or "miracle." He used it in a letter to a friend he was urging to accept Christianity, offering that miracles were the evidence of God's words. He defined a miracle as "anything which appears arduous or unusual, beyond the expectation or ability of the one who marvels at it."

> "Pray as though everything depended on God. Work as though everything depended on you."
> – **St. Augustine**

St. Augustine was ruthlessly candid and critical of himself in the autobiography chronicling his spiritual journey, *Confessions*. He thought that showing how God's mercy had never deserted him throughout his years of sin would encourage others to change their sinful ways. He pulled no punches about his own misdeeds and foolishness so that no one would regard him as being better than he really was. In fact, he explicitly detailed the weaknesses he was still struggling with.

"Fortitude is the disposition of soul which enables us to despise all inconveniences and the loss of things not in our power."
– St. Augustine

St. Augustine was canonized by acclamation, or by consensus, and there are no credible accounts of miracles performed during his lifetime. However, several people report having been cured of addictions and vices through the intercession of St. Augustine of Hippo. Some mothers, bemoaning the poor life choices of their adult children, report their offspring mending their sinful ways after their mothers prayed to St. Augustine and his mother, St. Monica, to help them find their way back to God.

B

> "He alone loves the Creator perfectly who manifests a pure love for his neighbor."
> **– St. Bede the Venerable**

Bede (673-735) was raised and educated in the Monastery of St. Paul in Jarrow, England, where he was instructed by the monks and became known as a great scholar of philosophy, astronomy, mathematics, grammar, ecclesiastical history, and theology. He was ordained as a deacon at 19 and as a priest at 30 and wrote prolifically. Except for a period of a few months spent teaching in the school of the archbishop of York, he spent his life in the monastery studying, writing, and praying. He gained acclaim for his *Ecclesiastical History of the English People*, which became the model for writing about history. Bede is also the first historian to establish the year of Christ's birth as the year 1 A.D. He is rare for having been venerated during his own lifetime.

> "Charity is that with which no man is lost, and without which no man is saved."
> **– St. Robert Bellarmine**

Born in Italy in 1542 to a devout mother, the half-sister of Pope Marcellus II (who held the office for less than a month), Robert entered the Society of Jesus at the age of eighteen. Once ordained, he began to teach and became a renowned scholar, serving as the chair of controversial theology and later Rector at the Roman College, as the Provincial of Naples, and eventually as Cardinal. He is best known for his defense of the Church against the anti-clericals and heretics of his time and for his influence in matters of church-state relations. His was a voice of reason in opposing harsh punishment for Galileo's support of the Copernican theory that the Earth revolves around the sun: "I say that if a real proof be found that the sun is fixed and does not revolve round the earth, but the earth round the sun, then it will be necessary, very carefully, to proceed to the explanation of the passages of Scripture which appear to be contrary, and we should rather say that we have misunderstood these than pronounce that to be false which is demonstrated." St. Robert Bellarmine died in 1621, and the process of canonization was initiated five years later, but it was not completed until 1930.

> "Prayer ought to be short and pure, unless it be prolonged by the inspiration of Divine grace."
> **– St. Benedict of Nursia**

Much of what is known of the life and works of St. Benedict comes from the biography written by St. Gregory, who was born three years before the death of the man who came to be known as the father of Western monasticism. When the young Benedict, born into privilege in central Italy in 480, was sent to Rome to complete his education, he was appalled by the way his classmates pursued pleasure and vice rather than truth. Fearing for his soul, he moved to a small village but soon felt compelled to seek solitude in the mountains, where he lived as a hermit in a cave. Feeling called to the fellowship of men who shared his values, he began to build a monastery north of Naples where monks would live, pray, work, and study in a community led by an Abbott. During the Middle Ages, the Rule of St. Benedict became the norm for monastic communities.

> "There is nothing better to display the truth in an excellent light, than a clear and simple statement of facts."
> **– St. Benedict of Nursia**

In his biography of St. Benedict, St. Gregory described Benedict's first miracle. When Benedict went to Rome to complete his education, he was accompanied by his childhood nurse, who had been his first teacher and loved him dearly, and when he fled the corruption of Rome, she went with him. In the village where they were staying, the nurse borrowed an earthenware sieve from a neighbor to clean some wheat. When she was done, she left the sieve on a table instead of returning it immediately, and it was accidentally broken in two. Benedict's nurse was very upset, and Benedict tried to console her. He took the broken sieve into another room and prayed over it fervently, asking God for it to be made whole again. When he rose from his knees, the sieve showed no sign of ever having been broken. The villagers were so amazed that they hung the sieve over the entrance to their church as proof of Benedict's grace and virtue.

"He who labors as he prays lifts his heart to God with his hands."
– **St. Benedict of Nursia**

St. Benedict's Rule makes clear his view of work as being a means to learning and maintaining self-discipline and obedience to God. It wasn't the type of work that mattered but rather the act of working, which prevents the idleness that can lead to sin. According to Benedict, work takes priority over everything, including prayer, because God's grace may not touch the heart and soul of an idler. In Benedict's time, manual labor was the lot of slaves and the low-born, but he considered it essential to being a Christian.

> "The nation doesn't simply need what we have. It needs what we are."
> – **St. Teresa Benedicta**

The youngest child of a large Jewish Polish family in 1891, at the age of 13 Edith Stein professed to no longer believe in God. She was an avid student of philosophy, and the autobiography of Theresa of Avila made such an impression on her that she studied Catholicism in earnest and was baptized a Catholic in 1922. Viewing scholarship as a service to God, she continued furthering her own education and teaching until the Nazis' Aryan Law banned anyone of Jewish descent from teaching. She became a Discalced Carmelite nun in Cologne in 1933 and took the name Teresa Benedicta of the Cross. By 1938, Jews in Germany were living under a reign of terror, and the prioress of the convent had Teresa smuggled across the border to a Carmelite convent in the Netherlands. She continued her studies and her writing there and was soon joined by her sister, Rosa, who had also converted and joined the Carmelites. During the Nazi occupation of Holland, Teresa Benedicta and her sister were arrested and sent to Auschwitz, along with several other Jews who had converted to Christianity. She died in the gas chamber in 1942 and was beatified by Pope John Paul II in 1987 and canonized in 1998.

"The want of proper examination, true contrition, and a firm purpose of amendment, is the cause of bad confessions, and of the ruin of souls."
– St. Benedict Joseph Labre

St. Benedict Joseph Labre is the patron saint of unmarried men, rejects, the mentally ill and insane, beggars, hobos, and the homeless. Born in France in 1748, he was the firstborn of 18 children. He was educated by his uncle, a parish priest, and from an early age wanted nothing more than to join a religious order. However, he was rejected by the Trappists, Carthusians, and Cistercians because he was sickly, and his academic preparation was considered inadequate for religious life. Giving up his goal of ordination, he set off on a pilgrimage throughout Europe that took him from one major shrine to the next, ending his journey several years later in Rome. Although he rarely begged, he earned the name, "The Beggar of Rome," for the years he spent living on the streets of the city and in the ruins of the Coliseum, surviving on food given to him or found in the city's trash heaps.

> "God is so good and so merciful, that to obtain Heaven it is sufficient to ask it of Him from our hearts."
> **– St. Benedict Joseph Labre**

St. Benedict Joseph Labre was filled with love of God and for the least fortunate of humanity. He lived on what was given to him and shared the little he had with the poor. When he became severely ill toward the end of his life, he sometimes accepted a bed in a hospice for poor men rather than sleeping in the ruins of the Coliseum, as he often did. On the day of his death in 1783, he made his way to a nearby church and prayed continuously for two hours. When he collapsed, he was carried to a neighboring house, where he died. Part of the house was later converted into a chapel housing his few possessions and a life-size statue marking the spot where he drew his last breath. Within months of his death at age 35, more than 130 miraculous cures attributed to his intercession had been recorded. Proclaimed a saint by the people shortly after his death, he was beatified in 1860 and canonized in 1881.

> "I want to follow you and be like you, O my Jesus; I would rather be crucified with you than enjoy all the pleasures of this world without you."
> **– St. Bernadette Soubirous**

Millions have made the pilgrimage to Lourdes, France seeking a cure for illness or infirmity. Thousands of cures have been documented since the 14-year old St. Bernadette experienced 16 visions of the Blessed Virgin between February 11 and March 25, 1858. The first vision occurred when Bernadette, accompanied by her younger sister and a friend, was sent to gather wood. Bernadette saw a beautiful young woman above a rose bush in the grotto of Massabielle. The apparition smiled at her and made the sign of the cross with a rosary, but Bernadette's sister and friend did not see the woman dressed in blue and white. During the girls' next visit to the grotto three days later, Bernadette fell into a trance upon seeing the apparition again, and during the third visit, on February 15, the vision asked Bernadette to return every day for the next two weeks, a period that became known as the "holy fortnight."

> "When you pass before a chapel and do not have time to stop for a while, tell your Guardian Angel to carry out your errand to Our Lord in the tabernacle. He will accomplish it and then still have time to catch up with you."
> **– St. Bernadette Soubirous**

During one of her visits to the grotto of Massabielle in Lourdes, young St. Bernadette was told by the apparition of the Holy Virgin to perform an act of atonement by drinking the water, washing in it, and eating the herb that grows there. Bernadette complied, and when she next returned she found that the grotto's formerly muddy water was clear and flowing freely. A few days later, the vision told her that a chapel should be built there. But it wasn't until the final visit, after Bernadette asked the lady's name three times, that the vision revealed herself as the Immaculate Conception. Not everyone believed Bernadette's accounts of her visions. Some thought she was delusional and still others thought she needed to do penance. Bernadette's story was subjected to intense scrutiny by both Church and state officials, and by 1862 they reached the conclusion that she spoke the truth. Since the local priest complied with Bernadette's request to build a chapel at the grotto, many churches have been built in the area, including the Basilica of St. Pius X.

"Love overcomes, love delights, those who love the Sacred Heart rejoice."
– St. Bernadette Soubirous

Bernadette shunned the attention she received once news of her visions and the subsequent miraculous cures spread, and she enrolled in the school operated by the Sisters of Charity of Nevers, where she finally learned to read and write. She subsequently entered the order and spent the remainder of her too-brief life at the motherhouse in Nevers working as an infirmary assistant and sacristan. Bernadette's health had been poor since a childhood case of cholera, and it deteriorated quickly after she was diagnosed with tuberculosis of the bone in her right knee. She regarded the great pain she suffered as penance and was praying the rosary when she died at the age of 35.

> "Everything is the Father's will: homeland, fortune, happiness, work, food, life, Jesus' death. Let His will be mine."
> **– St. Bernadette Soubirous**

One of the things that helped convince local officials that 14-year old Bernadette was telling the truth about her visions in the grotto of Massabielle was her report that the lady said finally revealed her name as the "Immaculate Conception." Those words had only recently been added by the pope to the teachings of the Church, and it was decided that it was extremely unlikely that the uneducated Bernadette would have been familiar with them. Consequently, it was concluded that she must have heard them from the Holy Virgin herself.

> "I believe though I do not comprehend, and I hold by faith what I cannot grasp with the mind."
> **– St. Bernard of Clairvaux**

From the earliest days of his religious life, St. Bernard of Clairvaux was known to perform miracles. Many of them were miraculous healings. For example, he prayed and made the sign of the cross over a young boy whose arm was paralyzed and withered, and the child's arm was immediately restored to normal appearance and function. Bernard also cured a man, a dear friend named Humbert, of epilepsy by praying over him. But not all the miracles attributed to St. Bernard were healings. It was reported that on the day of the dedication of the new church of the monastery he had founded in Leon, the church was filled with so many flies that their buzzing was a distraction from prayer. Bernard shouted out "Excommunicable eas!" and the flies all fell dead, so numerous that they had to be shoveled out of the church.

"When you covet that which delights you, think not only of the sweet moments of enjoyment, but of the long season of regret which must follow."
– **St. Bernard of Clairvaux**

St. Bernard figures prominently in 12th century European history. He was born into a noble and devout family in Burgundy, France. The faculty at the college where he studied theology and Holy Scripture at an early age were impressed by his piety, and when he decided to join the strict Cistercian Order in 1113, he convinced 30 young noblemen, including his brothers, to join with him. He was soon entrusted with the task of founding a monastery, the Abbey of Clairvaux, and was appointed to serve as Abbot. His reputation for austere holiness drew many new monks into the Abbey, including his own father and brothers. Over the next few years, Bernard founded several more monasteries, wrote prolifically, and became a trusted advisor sought out by both religious and secular authorities, all of which led to him being named as a Doctor of the Church in 1130. For his eloquence, he was given the title Doctor Mellifluus—the "honey-sweet doctor," and is the patron saint of beekeepers and candle makers.

"We are not innocent before God if we punish that which we should pardon, or pardon that which we should punish."
– St. Bernard of Clairvaux

As Doctor of the Church, Bernard traveled widely defending the rights of the Church against intrusion by secular rulers and acting as a negotiator and peacemaker during a time of schism within the Church. He played a key role in launching the Second Crusade by positioning taking the cross to gain absolution for sin. When the Crusade failed miserably, much of the blame fell on Bernard, who responded with the assertion that the crusaders themselves, through their sinful acts while on the march, were responsible for their own failure. He was already in failing health when he went on his last peacemaking trip in the spring of 1153, and he died shortly after his return, at the age of 63. During his 38 years as Abbott, 68 monasteries were established by the monks of Clairvaux. He was canonized in 1174 by Pope Alexander III.

> "Let each one ask of God grace for love of Jesus, notwithstanding that thou beest a sinner."
> **– St. Bernardine of Siena**

Pope Pius II referred to St. Bernadine as the "second Paul" for his tireless work in spreading the words of Jesus. Words mattered to Bernadine. He abhorred crude and shameful speech, yet he was not confident in his own speaking ability. He is as well known for his deeds before entering religious life as he is for his work as a Franciscan. In 1400, 20-year old Bernadine showed up to volunteer at the largest hospital in Siena, Italy, where a plague was claiming the lives of dozens of people every day. He simply wanted to help take care of the sick and dying, and he brought other young men in to do the same. Once the plague was over, he cared for his invalid aunt until her death, then joined the Franciscans and was ordained as a priest. He believed his voice to be too weak and hoarse for preaching and devoted his energy to prayer and his own spiritual growth. It was not until 12 years later, when he rose reluctantly to preach one day, that he spoke in a strong, clear voice. Listeners found his words so compelling that they made him promise to return to preach again. He became a fervent and indefatigable preacher, traveling all over Italy and attracting crowds of as many as 30,000 people. He did serve for a while as vicar general of his order, but during the last two years of his life he returned to preaching, which he had come to regard as his true calling.

> "The world would have peace if only men of politics would follow the Gospels."
> – **St. Birgitta of Sweden**

Since childhood, Birgitta had dream-visions showing her great things that God wanted her to do and messages for her to deliver to Church and secular leaders. As was the custom in the Middle Ages, she was married at 13 and bore eight children. Kinswoman to the King of Sweden, she served as lady-in-waiting to his young queen. After the death of her husband when she was 41, Birgitta prayed for guidance and was called by God to found a new religious order for women. The Lord's instructions were very detailed, down to the design and construction of the abbey church, the number of nuns, the clothing they were to wear, the prayers they were to say, and more. Before remodeling of the building donated by the king got very far, Jesus told Birgitta in a vision to go to Rome and remain there until she got the Pope to return from France. Though she obeyed, she was unsuccessful in getting the Pope to return or in ending the conflict between France and England. In fact, she didn't live to see any of God's messages that she delivered produce results. She was, however, canonized in 1391, and the monastic Augustinian order she founded for women, Ordo Sanctissimi Salvatoris (commonly referred to as the Brigittine or Bridgettine Order), spread throughout Europe.

> "While the world changes, the cross stands firm."
> **– St. Bruno**

St. Bruno is best known for his role in establishing the Carthusian order. Having spent his early religious life in Rheims as professor of theology and subsequently as head of the Cathedral school, he was named chancellor of Rheims by the archbishop, Manasses. When Manasses was denounced and later deposed, Bruno rejected the people's desire to appoint him archbishop, choosing instead life as a hermit. He and six companions settled in Grenoble in 1084, to establish a hermitage on land provided by the bishop in an isolated, mountainous area. They based the Carthusian Order roughly on the rule of St. Benedict, living in poverty and devoting themselves to work, prayer, and the transcription of manuscripts. Though he is regarded as a saint, Bruno was never canonized because formal canonization would have been antithetical to the Carthusians' rejection of formal recognition or honors.

"God never deserts a man, unless He is deserted by that man first. For even if a man shall have committed grievous sins once, twice, and a third time, God still looks for him, so that he may be converted and live."
– **St. Caesarius of Arles**

St. Caesarius (470-529) was ahead of his times in some ways. More than 250 of his sermons have survived and reveal his belief that the life of a Christian should involve reading the Scriptures, which means that developing public literacy was a worthy undertaking. He encouraged those who could read, clergy and laity alike, to help those who couldn't. He urged the illiterate to hire someone to read to them, and he had his works translated into several languages. Caesarius also believed that women should have equal opportunity to a monastic life, built a monastery for women outside of Arles, France, and established the first rule written specifically for women. His "Rule for Virgins" outlines the regimen to be maintained by women from the moment they enter the monastery until their death. A third way in which Caesarius was forward-thinking was in his recognition that Roman civilization was being replaced by European civilization. He envisioned a "world-embracing, world-uniting" society that would resonate with many people today.

"So blessed are you if you persevere in doing good, neither seeking nor desiring any consolation, for as St. Bernard says: To serve God is nothing else than to do good and suffer evil, and the rule of the true servant of Christ is never to receive consolation except in time of great necessity. This is the secure way; for whoever wants to go to God through sweetness and consolation is deceived."
– **St. Catherine of Bologna**

Catherine de'Vigri was born in 1413 in Bologna, Italy, the daughter of a diplomat to the Marquis of Ferrara, who was a member of the royal family. She spent part of her childhood at court as lady in waiting to the Marquis' wife and companion to his daughter, receiving an education befitting a member of the aristocracy. Catherine excelled in her studies and would become known for her skill as a painter and writer. At 13, after the Marquis had his wife executed for infidelity, Catherine chose religious life over life at court and joined a lay sisterhood in Ferrara. In 1431, the sisterhood was re-established as a convent of the Order of Poor Clares—the convent of Corpus Domini, where Catherine found fulfillment in the humblest of tasks and gained the admiration of her peers for her devoutness. She remained there as Mistress of Novices until 1456, when she was asked to return to Bologna and become Abbess of a new convent of Corpus Domini in that city. She held that position until her death in 1463.

"The fifth weapon is to remind oneself that we must die. This time is called the time of mercy in which God looks down day after day so that we can amend our lives from good to better. If we do not do this, we will have to render account, not only of the evils we have done, but also of the goods left undone by our negligence."
– **St. Catherine of Bologna**

Catherine wrote several treatises, poetry, and spiritual guides. A mystic, she had frequent visions throughout her life, some of which she described in her best-known work, "Treatise on the 7 Spiritual Weapons Necessary for Spiritual Warfare." Some of her visions were uplifting, such as her visions of the Blessed Mother and of Christ upon the cross, but she also had frightening visions of Satan. Interestingly, Catherine's father, Giovanni Vigri, a devout man, had a vision prior to his daughter's birth. In his vision, the Blessed Virgin, told him that his child would be a light in the world.

"So blessed are you if you persevere in doing good, neither seeking nor desiring any consolation, for as St. Bernard says: 'To serve God is nothing else than to do good and suffer evil, and the rule of the true servant of Christ is never to receive consolation except in time of great necessity.' This is the secure way; for whoever wants to go to God through sweetness and consolation is deceived."
– **St. Catherine of Bologna**

Catherine grew ill and died in March, 1463 and, in the tradition of her order, was buried without a coffin in the convent graveyard. People in the vicinity noticed a sweet scent emanating from her grave, and after 18 days, her body was exhumed. It was found to be without corruption, with the sweet scent coming from beads of what appeared to be sweat on the veil covering the face. The body was placed in the chapel next to the Corpus Domini convent, where it remains today, behind glass, seated on a throne and dressed in the habit of the Poor Clares. Although the skin has darkened from centuries of smoke and soot from burning candles and oil lamps, it remains as smooth and supple as it was in life. Adored for her piety and the miraculous cures attributed to her, St. Catherine was canonized in 1712 and is the patron saint of artists, the liberal arts, and the city of Bologna, as well as against temptation.

> "Confidence in God ought to be greater in proportion to the pressing nature of the necessity in which we are placed. When Jesus cried in the anguish of His Passion, 'My God, my God, why hast Thou forsaken me?' He was at that time exhibiting a pattern of the highest perfection in the exact fulfillment of the obedience required from Him by His Eternal Father, with Whom He was wholly united."
> – **St. Catherine of Bologna**

One of the miracles of St. Catherine of Bologna is sometimes called the "miracle of the baking bread." Catherine took great pleasure in baking the daily bread for the convent, but one day the bell calling the sisters to worship rang at a very inopportune time, when she had just put the bread in the oven to bake. Not knowing how long it would be before she could get back to the oven, she made the sign of the Cross over the loaves and commended them to the Lord. When she returned five hours later, believing the bread would have been burned to a crisp, she was surprised to find every loaf to be perfectly baked.

"Have not the boldness to say: 'I will go to confession and gain a plenary indulgence and thus I shall be saved.' Remember that the full confession and entire contrition which are requisite to gain a plenary indulgence are not easily attained. Did you know how hardly they are come by, you would tremble with fear and be more sure of losing than of gaining them."
– St. Catherine of Genoa

St. Catherine was born into Genoa's nobility as Caterina Fieschi Adorno in 1447. She tried to enter a convent at 13 but was deemed too young. Her parents arranged her marriage at 16 to a nobleman who made her life miserable with his philandering and selfishness. She sought escape in self-indulgent pursuits, though she never lost her faith. One day at confession she had a revelation of God's love and of her own sinful behavior. It filled her heart with grace, and her faith grew until her example of piety enabled her husband to reform his own life. Unfortunately, his profligacy had left them virtually penniless. Husband and wife decide to move into a large hospital in Genoa and devote themselves to caring for the sick and dying.

"Therefore God says to this proud man: If thou seekest, according to the nature of the created soul, for such great things as seem at present to be good and for that happiness which belongs to earth, know that they are not. They cannot satisfy nor afford contentment. Seek rather in heaven, where pride is lawful, and where it is not placed in things empty and vain, but in those which are really great, which always remain, and which cause a sinless pride. But if thou seekest after worthless things thou shalt never find them and shalt lost those which thou shouldst have sought.'"

– St. Catherine of Genoa

Catherine and her husband, bankrupted by his wasteful spending during his earlier years of sinful living, moved into a Genoa hospital where they would spend the rest of their lives doing good for those who suffered. They cared tirelessly for the sick and dying, exhausting themselves during the years of plague that ravaged the population. Catherine still found time for prayer and religious exercises, and she came to be known as a mystic because of the deep reveries she would often fall into while working. Catherine continued on her own after her husband's death in 1497, managing the women's division of the hospital until her own death. The treatises she wrote, particularly her treatise on purgatory, helped establish her reputation for holiness. St. Catherine of Genoa was canonized in 1737 by Pope Clement XII.

> "If you are what you should be, you will set the whole world ablaze!"
> **– St. Catherine of Sienna**

St. Catherine's entrance into religious life was a little unusual. Born the daughter of a prosperous and pious wool dyer in 1347 during an outbreak of the plague, she was the last of the couple's 25 children, half of whom died in infancy or early childhood. When her elder, married sister died at the age of 16, Catherine's parents pressured her to marry the widower, but Catherine believed she was meant for a religious life and finally convinced her parents to let her follow her calling. Because of her devotion to her family, she chose to join the Sisters of Penitence of the Third Order of St. Dominic rather than enter a convent. This allowed her to live a life of quiet isolation at home and still serve others, which she did primarily by giving her family's food and possessions to the needy. At 21, Catherine had what she called a "mystical marriage to Christ," which occurred in a vision that told her to give up her isolation and continue helping the needy in a more public manner. She ministered to the sick and the poor wherever they were to be found, gaining several followers in the process. Her mission would continue to evolve and expand far beyond what she had originally anticipated.

> "Frequently men lose time in longing for time to suit themselves, for they do not employ what they have otherwise than in suffering and gloominess."
> **– St. Catherine of Siena**

Once Catherine of Siena ventured out into the world on her mission to serve the needy, she started to travel and became more and more politically active. She encouraged Church reform, but she also spoke to the hearts of her followers and listeners, helping them learn to love God without reservation. At a time when the Italian city-states were questioning papal authority, she spoke out to help maintain their loyalty. She wrote letters advocating for peace among the city-states and played a key role in getting the pope to return from Avignon to Rome.

"Proclaim the truth and do not be silent through fear."
– St. Catherine of Siena

Throughout her life, Catherine of Siena practiced extreme fasting and other mortifications of the flesh as penance to bring herself closer to God. She scourged herself three times a day to atone for her own sins, the sins of the living, and those of souls in purgatory. She cinched an iron chain around her body so tightly that it bit into her flesh. She deprived herself not only of food but also of sleep, allowing herself to rest for only half an hour each night, and toward the end of her life she denied herself any sleep at all.

"There is no sin nor wrong that gives a man such a foretaste of hell in this life as anger and impatience. It is hated by God, it holds its neighbor in aversion, and has neither knowledge nor desire to bear and forbear with its faults. And whatever is said or done to it, it at once empoisons, and its impulses blow about like a leaf in the wind."
– **St. Catherine of Siena**

During her lifetime, Catherine was known as a mystic. Witnesses reported seeing her float up the stairs in her home as a young child, without putting a foot on a step, and she is said to have experienced her first vision at age 6. She said that when she looked up to the sky that day, she saw Christ sitting on a heavenly throne flanked by Saints Peter, Paul, and John. He was wearing a bishop's robes and blessed her with the Sign of the Cross. When she had her vision of her mystical marriage to Christ, she claimed to have been given a wedding ring that was apparently visible only to her. Similarly, she reportedly bore the stigmata, though only she could see them.

> "Prayer is a pasturage, a field, wherein all the virtues find their nourishment, growth, and strength."
> **– St. Catherine of Siena**

In 1377, St. Catherine founded a women's monastery on the outskirts of Siena. As a writer, her major work was her "Dialogue," consisting of more than 400 letters. Many of them were dictated to scribes. Her prayers were also highly regarded. It is largely because of her writing that St. Catherine was declared a Doctor of the Church in 1970 by Pope Paul VI. She was only the second woman to receive this honor, St. Theresa of Avila receiving it only a week earlier.

"Eternal Trinity, Godhead, mystery deep as the sea, you could give me no greater gift than the gift of yourself. For you are a fire ever burning and never consumed, which itself consumes all the selfish love that fills my being. Yes, you are a fire that takes away the coldness, illuminates the mind with its light, and causes me to know your truth. And I know that you are beauty and wisdom itself. The food of angels, you gave yourself to man in the fire of your love."
– **St. Catherine of Siena**

Catherine became ill at the beginning of 1380, but she continued to refuse food even when her confessor urged her to eat. Her condition deteriorated rapidly, her decline most likely hastened by her lifelong habit of extreme fasting and sleep deprivation. She soon lost the use of her legs, suffered a stroke in April, and died a week later at the same age as Christ when he went to the Cross. She was canonized in 1461 by Pope Pius II, also from Siena.

"We must meditate before, during, and after everything we do. The prophet says: 'I will pray, and then I will understand.' This is the way we can easily overcome the countless difficulties we have to face day after day, which, after all, are part of our work. In meditation we find the strength to bring Christ to birth in ourselves and in others."
– **St. Charles Borromeo**

When Charles Borromeo declared his intention at age 12 to serve the Church, he was given an income by his maternal uncle, Cardinal Giovanni Angelo Medici, but Charles insisted that all but the amount needed to fund his education was to be given to the poor. His uncle became Pope Pius IV in 1559, which determined the trajectory of Charles Borromeo's life. Barely out of his teens at the time, Charles had already earned a doctorate in canon and civil law and had been supporting his family since the death of his father, the Count of Arona. With such proof of Charles's integrity as the charitable disposal of his income, his uncle brought him to Rome and made him a cardinal-deacon and elevated him to cardinal only a month later.

> "If we wish to make any progress in the service of God we must begin every day of our life with new eagerness. We must keep ourselves in the presence of God as much as possible and have no other view or end in all our actions but the divine honor."
> **– St. Charles Borromeo**

Among Charles's responsibilities as cardinal were advising his uncle, Pope Pius IV, governing the Papal States, and supervising the Knights of Malta, the Franciscans, and the Carmelites. Still in his early twenties, he became administrator of the Archdiocese of Milan, which prompted him to seek ordination. Even as he prepared for the priesthood, he promoted learning and founded a college at Pavia. Within a span of less than two years, Charles was ordained as a deacon, then as a priest, and three months later as a bishop, becoming Archbishop of Milan in 1564. His rapid rise in the Church might be described today as meteoric.

"Behold Jesus Christ crucified, who is the only foundation of our hope; he is our mediator and advocate; the victim and sacrifice for our sins. He is goodness and patience itself; his mercy is moved by the tears of sinners, and he never refuses pardon and grace to those who ask it with a truly contrite and humbled heart."
– **St. Charles Borromeo**

Archbishop Borromeo's mission in Milan, the largest diocese in the Church in his day, was to root out corruption and stem the tide of the Protestant Reformation that was sweeping across Europe. He firmly believed that the answer lie in reforming the Catholic Church, largely through the education of clergy, many of whom were ill-informed on Church doctrine. In addition to establishing seminaries and religious colleges, Archbishop Borromeo curtailed some of the practices that Protestants found most objectionable, such as selling indulgences. He ordered churches to remove excessive decorative elements, which Protestants viewed as distractions from worship, and simplify their interiors. His zeal in rooting out corruption, however, was not universally appreciated within the Church.

"He who serves God with a pure heart, laying aside all human interests and seeking only the divine honor, may hope to succeed in his affairs even when to others they seem desperate, since the operations of God are beyond the ken of mortal vision, and depend on a loftier than human policy."
– **St. Charles Borromeo**

Archbishop Borromeo ignored the complaints of those who opposed his efforts to eliminate corruption in the Church and survived a failed assassination attempt. In fact, opposition only strengthened his resolve. In the last two years of his life, he extended his focus to heresy in Switzerland and travelled there in response to reports of witchcraft. Ever a believer in the power of education to bring about meaningful reform, he established a college for the education of Swiss Catholics. When he became ill in 1584, Archbishop Borromeo returned to Milan, where he died at only 46 years of age. Pope Paul V beatified him in 1602 and canonized him in 1610. St. Charles Borromeo is the patron of bishops, catechists, cardinals, seminarians, and spiritual leaders.

"The prayer of the sick person is his patience and his acceptance of the sickness for the love of Jesus Christ. This has great worth when it is motivated by the imitation of how much Our Lord suffered for us, and by penance for our sins."
– **St. Charles of Sezze**

The young John Charles Marchioni was not a person anyone would have thought would one day be canonized. Born in Sezze, Italy in 1630, he was a shepherd who wanted nothing more than to serve God as a priest. His lack of education prevented him from becoming a priest, but he served as a lay brother for most of his adult life. The positions he held in every monastery he served in were menial, and his life was simple. Despite his lack of formal education, he wrote about his mystical experiences and was highly regarded for his holiness and charity. Though Charles died in Rome, he is known as Charles of Sezze, the place of his birth. He died in 1670 and was canonized by Pope John XXIII in 1959.

"Despise temptations against the faith and remember that you believe what so many saints and doctors have believed."
— **St. Claude de la Colombiere**

Claude de la Colombiere was born in 1641 and died 41 years later. Two months after his ordination in 1675, Claude was appointed superior of a small Jesuit residence in Burgundy, France. In that position, he met Margaret Mary Alacoque, who would eventually be canonized herself. She became Claude's spiritual companion, and he served as her confessor for many years. Claude was known for his preaching skills and for his success in converting Protestants to Catholicism. Throughout his life he preached about and exemplified God's love for all. He was sent to England to be confessor to the Duchess of York during a period of rising anti-Catholic sentiments. Claude was imprisoned on suspicion of being part of a conspiracy against the king and was in ill health by the time he was banished from England. St. Claude de la Colombiere was canonized in 1992 by Pope John Paul II.

> "We should let God be the One to praise us and not praise ourselves. For God detests those who commend themselves. Let others applaud our good deeds."
> – **Pope St. Clement I**

The life and acts of St. Clement I are largely shrouded in the mists of history. Among the few facts that can be confirmed is his status as a disciple of St. Peter. There is some confusion as to whether Clement was the immediate successor of St. Peter, as some sources place him as the fourth bishop of Rome rather than the second. One likely explanation is that there were initially two lines of succession, one from St. Peter and the other from St. Paul, with the Petrine line governing Jewish converts and the Pauline line the Gentile converts. It's believed that Clement may have succeeded St. Peter while Linus and Cletus were the next Pauline bishops. With the merger of the two lines, the enumeration of the bishops of Rome would depend on whether the Pauline bishops were counted. The only reliable information about the life and works of St. Clement I comes from one surviving letter he wrote that speaks of a schism in the Church at Corinth. Though some Church historians refer to Pope St. Clement I as a martyr, others do not. There are no reliable accounts of the manner of his death, though it is believed to have occurred around the year 100 A.D.

> "This world and the world to come are two enemies. We cannot therefore be friends to both; but we must decide which we will forsake and which we will enjoy."
> **– Pope St. Clement I**

Though few facts are known about Pope St. Clement I, he has been the subject of much speculation and storytelling over the centuries. Legend has it that there was a popular uprising among the lower classes of Rome against the Christians during Clement's reign as Bishop of Rome. The prefect of the city quelled the rioting and had Clement arrested and sent to the emperor, Trajan, who sentenced him to labor in the marble quarries. Thus, Clement is known as the patron saint of marble workers.

"Charity unites us to God… There is nothing mean in charity, nothing arrogant. Charity knows no schism, does not rebel, does all things in concord. In charity all the elect of God have been made perfect."
– **Pope St. Clement I**

While the actual circumstances of Clement's death are unknown, legend has it that he was condemned to die by drowning because of his success in converting pagans to Christianity. He was reportedly thrown into the sea with an anchor tied around his neck, and one of his disciples retrieved his body. Paintings of St. Clement show him dressed in papal robes standing beside an anchor.

> "If there be a true way that leads to the Everlasting Kingdom, it is most certainly that of suffering, patiently endured."
> **– St. Colette**

After being orphaned at 17, Nicolette de Boilet gave her inheritance to the poor and entered religious life as a Franciscan tertiary. For four years beginning at age 21, she lived as an anchoress, or solitary, walled into a room with only one opening: a window into a church sanctuary. She left her cell only after having a dream in which she was told to reform the Poor Clares. The church was still divided by the Great Schism, and there was much concern that those in religious life had strayed from their rule. The Avignon pope, Benedictine XIII, supported Colette's mission to establish new monasteries following the primitive Rule of St. Clare. Because of two miracles that occurred during her lifetime—one that resulted in a safe delivery and the other through which a newborn was restored to life, St. Colette is the patron saint of expectant mothers and sick children, as well as of women seeking to conceive. She was canonized in 1807.

> "Nothing is sweeter than the calm of conscience, nothing safer than purity of soul - yet no one can bestow this on himself because it is properly the gift of God's grace."
> – **St. Columban**

St. Columban was an Irish missionary who, with a small group of fellow missionaries from Ireland, established several monasteries in different parts of Europe. He is credited for several miracles during his lifetime (543-615), including: being left untouched by a pack of wolves; producing a spring of water; multiplying food and drink; restoring a blind man's sight; taming a bear and getting it to pull a plow; replenishing a village's empty granary, and more. When in Bregrenz during a famine, the Irish missionary prayed for food after three days with nothing to eat, and the ground was suddenly covered by birds that did not fly away but rather allowed themselves to be scooped up for food. The "manna" of birds remained until a supply of grain arrived on the fourth day, sent by a priest in a nearby city who had been told in a vision to send relief to St. Columban. When the birds were no longer needed, they flew away en masse.

> "I am innocent, and I die innocent. I forgive with all my heart those responsible for my death, and I ask God that the shedding of my blood serves toward the peace of our divided Mexico."
> – **St. Cristobal**, just before his executioners fired

St. Cristobal, son of a farmer, became a parish priest in Totatiche, Mexico during a time of growing anti-Church sentiment in the government. He worked tirelessly on behalf of the people, helping establish schools, catechism centers, and a newspaper to educate and inform them. He also helped establish carpentry shops and a power plant to provide employment and spur economic development. He brought together indigenous people from the countryside with the townspeople in agricultural cooperatives that benefited both. The closure of seminaries by the government propelled Father Cristobal into actions that would be interpreted by those in power as support of the Cristero guerilla revolt, though his goal was to dissuade the people from taking up arms against the government. He was arrested in May 1927, and he was sentenced to death without a trial. While in prison, he absolved his executioners before being martyred by firing squad, along with St. Agustin Caloca.

> Nothing seems tiresome or painful when you are working for a Master who pays well; who rewards even a cup of cold water given for love of Him.
> – **St. Dominic Savio**

Dominic Savio was born into a poor family of devout Catholics and was raised from the age of two in the village now known as Castlenuovo Don Bosco for its proximity to the birthplace of John Bosco. Dominic displayed an unusual piety from early childhood and was brought to the attention of Father Bosco (later canonized himself) by his teacher. Falsely accused by his teacher based on the lies of two students trying to escape punishment for their own misdeed, Dominic did not defend himself. When the teacher learned the truth and asked Dominic why he hadn't denied the accusation, the boy said that he was emulating Jesus, who remained silent when unjustly accused. Father Bosco was impressed with Dominic's knowledge of Catholicism and determination to become a priest and ensured his admission to the secondary school in Turin, where he became the boy's teacher and mentor. After writing a report on sainthood, Dominic announced his own desire to become a saint. Dominic was 14 when he became ill and was sent home to recover, and though his doctor believed he would get better, Dominic was certain of his own impending death. Father Bosco felt the boy's loss deeply and wrote a book about Dominic's life of unusual piety and devotion. Venerated in 1933, beatified in 1950, and canonized in 1954, St. Dominic Savio became the youngest non-martyr ever to become a saint. He is the patron of choirboys, the falsely accused, and juvenile delinquents.

> "It is better to say one 'Our Father' fervently and devoutly than a thousand with no devotion and full of distraction."
> – **St. Edmund**

Born in 840, Edmund became king of East Anglia when he was about 14. He was martyred in 870 when he refused to accept the terms demanded by the conquering Danes—terms he felt bound as a Christian to reject. (He felt so strongly about prayer that he had once retired to his royal tower and dedicated a year to committing the entire Psalter to memory.) To prevent the slaughter of his troops, he disbanded them after a crushing defeat and was travelling on his own when he was captured by the invading Danes and brought before the Viking king, Hinguar. Edmund again rejected the demands he deemed impious, choosing his religion over his life. He was beaten and scourged, but he clung unwaveringly to his faith. His torturers, angered by his persistence, shot arrows into his body until Hinguar ordered him to be decapitated by sword. His relics were removed from his original burial place in the tenth century to a town that has since been re-named St. Edmundsbury. He is the patron of torture victims and the Roman Catholic diocese of East Anglia, among other people, places, and causes.

> "You well know that I preferred his company to all the delights of the world. But since it has pleased You to take him from me, I accept Your will completely."
> – **St. Elizabeth Ann Seton** (on the death of her husband)

Elizabeth found consolation in the fact that her husband had come to know God before he died. Having been born into New York's high society, Elizabeth married the wealthy William Seton in 1794. It was a true love match, and the first four years of the marriage were happy and trouble-free. During that period, Elizabeth Ann Seton became one of the founders of the first charitable institution in New York City, the Society for the Relief of Widows with Small Children. Little did she know she would soon become one herself. The Setons' love endured through the difficult times that followed the death of William's father, which left the young couple with full responsibility for running the family's business and raising his seven half-siblings. Their bond grew even stronger as William's health deteriorated and as he was forced to declare bankruptcy. The Setons moved to Italy, where William had business friends, to improve his declining health. After his death from tuberculosis, Elizabeth moved her family back to the United States.

> "If I had to advise parents, I should tell them to take great care about the people with whom their children associate ... Much harm may result from bad company, and we are inclined by nature to follow what is worse than what is better."
> **– St. Elizabeth Ann Seton**

Elizabeth Ann Bayley, born in 1774, was the daughter of a wealthy New York physician, but found more pleasure in reading and quiet pursuits than in the usual high society pastimes. Always fond of reading the Scriptures, her interest in the Bible and her reliance on it for comfort grew and became her bedrock in difficult times. Widowed at an early age and a convert to Catholicism, Elizabeth Ann Seton accepted an invitation from the president of St. Mary's College to come to Baltimore and open a school for Catholic girls. She was joined by several young women in founding the first American-based sisterhood, and they took their vows in 1809. Elizabeth was thereafter known as Mother Seton. The rule the sisterhood adopted made accommodations for her to continue raising her children. The sisterhood later moved to Emmitsburg, Maryland, where they educated the poor girls of the parish at no cost to the families. This is widely regarded as the birth of Catholic parochial education in America. In 1812, the sisterhood became the Sisters of Charity of St. Joseph and began opening new houses. By the time Mother Seton died, the order had 20 communities.

"I will go peaceably and firmly to the Catholic Church: for if Faith is so important to our salvation, I will seek it where true Faith first began, seek it among those who received it from God Himself."
– **St. Elizabeth Ann Seton**

Adversity and the loss of loved ones grew Elizabeth closer and closer to God, but she didn't become a Catholic until friends in Italy, where she and her husband were living at the time of his death, guided her in the direction she had already chosen for her life. Having endured so much, she found comfort in embracing God's will, and she longed to know Him better. She came to regard the Blessed Virgin as her own true mother, having lost her earthly mother as a child. Elizabeth studied Catholicism for months and joined the Catholic Church in 1805 in New York City, shortly after the Colonial Anti-Catholic laws were lifted.

"We know certainly that our God calls us to a holy life. We know that he gives us every grace, every abundant grace; and though we are so weak of ourselves, this grace is able to carry us through every obstacle and difficulty."
– St. Elizabeth Ann Seton

From her early forties, Mother Elizabeth Seton had a sense that God would soon be calling her, and she looked forward to it with joyful anticipation. Ironically, she would succumb to tuberculosis, as her beloved husband William had years earlier. She was 46 when she died in 1821, having been a Catholic for only 16 years. She was beatified by Pope John XXIII in 1963 and was canonized by Pope Paul VI twelve years later, becoming the first American-born saint. She is the patron of in-law problems, against the death of children, widows, death of parents, and opposition of Church authorities.

> "I know well that the greater and more beautiful the work is, the more terrible will be the storms that rage against it."
> **– St. Faustina**

Helena Kowalska, born into a poor but devout family near Lodz, Poland in 1905, was only seven when she felt called to religious life. She was still a teenager when she had her first vision of a suffering Jesus and reported that He told her to leave for Warsaw right away and enter a convent. Turned away by all the convents she approached, she finally found one that would accept her on the condition that she pay for her own habit, which she did by working as a housekeeper. At age 20, Helena entered the Congregation of the Sisters of Our Lady of Mercy, took the name Sister Maria Faustina of the Blessed Sacrament.

> "He who knows how to forgive prepares for himself many graces from God. As often as I look upon the cross, so often will I forgive with all my heart."
> **– St. Faustina**

By 1931, Faustina was showing signs of the tuberculosis that she would battle for the remainder of her too-short life. That same year, Faustina had another vision of Jesus, who appeared to her as the "King of Divine Mercy" and asked her to become an instrument for sharing God's mercy in the world. She wrote in her diary that Jesus asked her to paint an image of Him as he appeared to her with the inscription, "Jesus, I trust in you." She described Him as being dressed in a white robe and having red and white rays of light emanating from his chest. Faustina had no artistic talent or skills, but eventually found an artist to create the painting for her.

> "The greatest misery does not stop Me from uniting Myself to a soul, but where there is pride, I am not there."
> – **St. Faustina** (the words of Jesus as recorded in her diary)

Soon after taking her final vows as a perpetual sister of Our Lady of Mercy, Faustina told her confessor, Father Sopocko, about her visions and the plan Jesus had for her. Father Sopocko decided to support her in executing that plan, but only after she passed a psychiatric examination. He encouraged her to keep a written record of all her visions and the instructions she received from Jesus. In 1935, a week after Faustina had a vision in which Jesus told her he wanted the Divine Mercy painting to be honored publicly, Father Sopocko delivered the first sermon on the Divine Mercy.

"I [urge] all souls to trust in the unfathomable abyss of My mercy, because I want to save them all. On the cross, the fountain of My mercy was opened wide by the lance for all souls - no one have I excluded!"
– **St. Faustina** (the words of Jesus as recorded in her diary)

Faustina continued to have visions in which Jesus gave her instructions for spreading the message of his Divine Mercy, and she did everything she could to obey. Her failing health forced her to enter a sanatorium, but in 1937, she lived to see the first holy cards bearing the Divine Mercy image distributed and become extremely popular. She also passed on the instructions she said that Jesus had given her for the Novena of Divine Mercy.

"We do not know the number of souls that is ours to save through our prayers and sacrifices; therefore, let us always pray for sinners."
– **St. Faustina**

Faustina wrote in her diary about her vision of hell, which she says God ordered her to visit so that she could tell others that it truly exists. She noted that most of the souls in hell were disbelievers in the existence of hell. She described the seven kinds of torture she witnessed in the abysses of hell, the first of which was the loss of God. Having seen firsthand the suffering of souls in hell, she prayed more intensely than ever for the conversion of sinners, writing "I incessantly plead God's mercy upon them."

"Let souls who are striving for perfection particularly adore My mercy, because the abundance of graces which I grant them flows from My mercy. I desire that these souls distinguish themselves by boundless trust in My mercy. I myself will attend to the sanctification of such souls. I will provide them with everything they will need to attain sanctity."
– **St. Faustina** (the words of Jesus as recorded in her diary)

Tuberculosis of the lungs and the gastrointestinal tract, exacerbated by her long habit of extreme fasting, caused Faustina great suffering. As her health continued to decline, Faustina's visions came more frequently until her death in October 1938. Healing miracles attributed to the intercession of Sister Faustina led to her being canonized as St. Faustina Kowalska in 2000 by Pope John Paul II. She is venerated as the "Apostle of Divine Mercy."

> "Mankind will not have peace until it turns with trust to My mercy."
> – **St. Faustina** (the words of Jesus as recorded in her diary)

Few people who knew Sister Faustina were aware of her mystical life. Her outward life was unremarkable, some might say insignificant. It was a life of service and obedience, and the occupations she was assigned were simple: cook, gardener, porter. She was regarded as kind and serene, and her appearance and conduct gave no hint of her inner life and her spiritual gifts, including visions, revelations, prophecy, hidden stigmata, and more, which she regarded as "merely ornaments of the soul." It was only in her later years, with the growth of devotion to the Divine Mercy, that she gained a reputation for having a special relationship with God.

> "Woe to me if I should prove myself but a halfhearted soldier in the service of my thorn-crowned Captain."
> – **St. Fidelis of Sigmaringen**

After several years of practicing law, Mark Rey, born in Sigmaringen, Prussia in 1577, had his fill of corruption and incivility and decided to become a Capuchin friar. He was given the religious name "Fidelis," meaning "faithful," and within a relatively short time he was assigned to be Guardian of a Capuchin friary in present-day Austria, followed by a preaching commission in eastern Switzerland. He and the friars assisting him were very successful in converting Calvinists, which earned Fidelis death threats from the remaining Calvinists. They claimed he was a spy for the Austrian emperor. Fidelis preached in a church in Seewis, Switzerland on Sunday, April 24, 1622. At the end of his sermon he fell into an ecstasy and awoke with the certainty that he would be martyred that day. Confronted on the road by 20 rebel Calvinist soldiers led by a minister, he refused their order to renounce Catholicism and was brutally stabbed and hacked to death. The minister leading the rebels later denounced Calvinism and became a Catholic.

> "We must pray without tiring, for the salvation of mankind does not depend on material success; nor on sciences that cloud the intellect. Neither does it depend on arms and human industries, but on Jesus alone."
> **– St. Frances Xavier Cabrini**

Maria Francesca Cabrini's health was fragile from the beginning with her premature birth in Lombardy, Italy in 1850 to her death in Chicago, Illinois eight years after becoming a naturalized U.S citizen. She was refused entry to the religious congregation of the Daughters of the Sacred Heart at age 18 because of her health, despite having received her education in the order's convent school. She spent six years teaching at the House of Providence Orphanage in Cadagono, Italy before she took her vows and became Mother Frances Xavier Cabrini. When the orphanage closed, at the request of the bishop, Mother Cabrini, along with several other sisters, founded the Missionary Sisters of the Sacred Heart to care for poor children in both schools and hospitals. Five years later, after helping found several homes and programs for children in Italy, Mother Cabrini wanted to do mission work in China, but Pope Leo XII urged her to go to the United States, instead, to help the many needy Italian immigrants there. In March 1899 she arrived in New York City with six other sisters, determined to succeed in their mission no matter what adversities they faced.

> "It is not the actual physical exertion that counts toward a man's progress, nor the nature of the task, but the spirit of faith with which it is undertaken."
> – **St. Frances Xavier Cabrini**

Mother Cabrini's first project in the United States was to found an orphanage in West Park, New York, which still exists and is now called the St. Cabrini Home. Using her talent for enlisting the support of others, Frances went on to found a total of 67 orphanages, schools, and hospitals to benefit the needy, especially Italian immigrants, in New York and elsewhere in the U.S. She died in 1917 at age 67 from complications of dysentery in a hospital she had founded in Chicago. Three years later, an infant born in New York's Columbus Hospital, founded by Mother Cabrini, was accidentally administered silver nitrate eye drops in a 50% concentration instead of the usual 1% solution. The resulting chemical burns, according to every expert, had caused permanent facial disfiguration and blindness. Told that only a miracle could save his vision, the sisters of the order founded by Mother Cabrini gathered in the hospital chapel and prayed throughout the night for her intercession with Jesus to heal the boy. The next morning, his charred skin was already healing, and his eyes showed no damage at all. A few hours later, he developed pneumonia, often a death sentence in the days before antibiotics. Once again, the sisters prayed through the night and by morning the pneumonia was gone. With these and other healing miracles attributed to her, Mother Cabrini was canonized in 1946.

> "What does the poor man do at the rich man's door, the sick man in the presence of his physician, the thirsty man at a limpid stream? What they do, I do before the Eucharistic God. I pray. I adore. I love."
> **– St. Francis of Assisi**

Pietro Bernadone's son was born in 1182 while the merchant was away on a trip to France, a country he was infatuated with. Upon returning home and finding that the boy had been baptized Giovanni, after John the Baptist, Pietro was furious and renamed him Francesco. He wanted his son to take over his business one day, not become a man of God. Young Francesco's life was an easy, privileged one, and everyone who met him liked him. He acquired a following of young people who indulged in wild and reckless behavior, though he later recognized this as a sinful period in his life.

"All the darkness in the world cannot extinguish the light of a single candle."
– **St. Francis of Assisi**

Young Francesco Bernadone shared his father's attraction to all things French, but he didn't want to go into business as his father wanted him to. Instead, he had dreams of nobility and knighthood. When he got a chance to go to battle in defense of Assisi as part of a militia group, he was captured and spent a year in a dungeon before he was ransomed. Undeterred by the experience, he answered the call to participate in the Fourth Crusade, riding out of Assisi clad in gold-trimmed armor and vowing to return as a prince. But a day later he turned around and rode home after dreaming that God told him to. He returned to face ridicule and accusations of cowardice, and the anger of his father over the money wasted on fancy armor.

> "Alms are an inheritance and a justice which is due to the poor and which Jesus has levied upon us."
> **– St. Francis of Assisi**

While praying in the church at Damiano one day, Francis heard Jesus on the crucifix call him by name and say to him, "Repair my church." Francis took merchandise from his father's business to sell for money to start repairing the ancient church building, without realizing that the message referred to the Church with a capital "C." Pietro, his father, was furious and hauled Francis in front of the bishop where he publicly demanded restitution for the stolen merchandise and disinherited his son. The bishop told Francis to make restitution and trust that God would provide. This was the pivotal moment in Francis's life. He not only returned the money, but also removed the clothes his father had paid for and announced that henceforth his only father was his Father in heaven. From that moment on, material possessions meant nothing to Francis, and his only desire was to serve God.

> "Sanctify yourself and you will sanctify society."
> **– St. Francis of Assisi**

It took Francis (the anglicized version of Francesco) a while to find his way to God. His dream in which God told him to turn back from his quest for glory as a crusading knight got him thinking. He started praying and repenting for the sins of his youth. He was clearly searching for answers and direction. But it was not until he overcame his distaste for ugliness and deformity and kissed the hand of a leper that he felt he had been tested by God and has passed.

With no formal religious training, Francis began preaching as he wandered from place to place, sleeping in the open and begging for scraps of food. His was a ministry of love, respecting all of God's creation and urging listeners to love God and obey the Church. He acquired several followers who wanted to live as he did—people from all walks of life, rich and poor, educated and ignorant, city dwellers and peasants from the countryside, nobles and commoners. They moved from place to place, sleeping in the open or in caves or lean-tos they fashioned from branches. Francis felt a responsibility to provide direction for them, though he had no interest in establishing a formal religious order. Rather, he thought of the growing group as a brotherhood that included all living creatures, animals as well as human beings.

"By the anxieties and worries of this life Satan tries to dull man's heart and make a dwelling for himself there."
– St. Francis of Assisi

Francis led by example and lived by the Gospel. He chose three passages to serve as the Rule for his brotherhood of God: Jesus' command to the rich man to sell all his possessions and give the money to the poor; His instructions to the apostles to leave everything behind; and the order to take up the cross daily.

> "It would be considered a theft on our part if we didn't give to someone in greater need than we are."
> **– St. Francis of Assisi**

Francis became known for his directness and complete lack of artifice. He acted instinctively, from an inner sense of what was right and what response a situation called for. Sometimes, this led to mistakes, which Francis was quick to recognize and correct. For example, he once ordered a brother who did not want to speak in public because of his stutter to go into town and preach half-naked. As soon as Francis realized the pain his command caused to someone he loved, Francis ran after him, took off his own clothes, and preached in his place.

> "Where there is hatred, let me sow love. Where there is injury, pardon. Where there is doubt, faith."
> **– St. Francis of Assisi**

After spending years in Syria converting Muslims during the Fifth Crusade, Francis returned to Italy to find that the brotherhood had grown to more than 5,000 brothers practicing radical poverty. He faced great criticism and demands that he impose some discipline and structure on the organization. Many in the Church believed that the brotherhood needed a Rule that conformed to what was more in line with the standards of more traditional religious orders. Francis gave up his leadership role, apparently content to be one brother among many. Today he is regarded as the founder of all Franciscan orders.

> "Every day, Jesus humbles Himself just as He did when He came from His heavenly throne into the Virgin's womb; everyday He comes to us and lets us see Him in abjection, when He descends from the bosom of the Father into the hands of the priest at the altar."
> **– St. Francis of Assisi**

In his later years, Francis suffered the physical consequences of years of living in radical poverty. He regarded his suffering from malaria as an opportunity to share in Christ's passion, and he had a vision of his own body marked with the stigmata of Christ's wounds. He was also losing his eyesight. The 13th century treatment for preventing blindness was a brutal one that involved cauterizing the patient's face with a hot iron. Francis prayed to "Brother Fire" to be merciful and reported when the procedure was over that he had felt no pain at all. During his years of illness, a childhood friend named Clare, founder of the Poor Clares, helped nurse him.

"Heaven open, Hell open, between the two is the Christian."
– St. Francis of Assisi

Francis died in 1226 and was canonized only two years late due in large part to the many miracles attributed to him during his lifetime. He is credited with healing people in body and soul. He was also observed to tame a ferocious wolf, one known to have killed livestock and people, by making the sign of the Cross, praying over it, and speaking to it with loving kindness, assuring it that the local residents would feed it regularly. The wolf never killed again. It was also reported that flocks of birds would gather around Francis to listen to him preach. Fittingly, St. Francis is the patron of animals.

"Recall yourself sometimes to the interior solitude of your heart, and there, removed from all creatures, treat of the affairs of your salvation and your perfection with God, as a friend would speak heart to heart with another."
– St. Francis de Sales

Francis was born into nobility in 1567 in the Kingdom of Savoy, France, not far from Geneva, Switzerland. As is often the case, father and son had very different plans for Francis' life. His father, a member of the senate, expected Francis to follow in his footsteps and take his place in the senate one day. Francis, from an early age, felt a calling to the priesthood. It was confirmed when he fell from his horse three times while out riding one day. Each time he fell, his sword came out of its scabbard and the two landed on the ground, one on top of the other, in the shape of the cross. Francis didn't reveal his calling to his parents until after he had received his doctorate in law from the University of Padua. His father was strongly opposed to the idea but eventually gave his consent. Francis was ordained by the Bishop of Geneva and elected provost of the Diocese of Geneva in 1593.

"Depend upon it, it is better to learn how to live without being angry than to imagine one can moderate and control anger lawfully; and if through weakness and frailty one is overtaken by it, it is far better to put it away forcibly than to parley with it; for give anger ever so little way, and it will become master, like the serpent, who easily works in its body wherever it can once introduce its head."
– **St. Francis de Sales**

A story about Francis de Sales as a young child provides insight to his early devotion to the Catholic faith and to the quick temper that took twenty years to tame. A group of visitors arrived at his family's chateau one day, and some of them were Calvinists. Upon learning this, Francis, too young to join the gathering inside the chateau, grabbed a stick and chased the chickens around the courtyard, yelling at them and calling them out as Calvinists. Fortunately, as provost of the Diocese of Geneva, and later as Bishop, his efforts to convert Calvinists relied on gentle words and patience rather than a big stick.

"Make yourself familiar with the Angels, and behold them frequently in spirit. Without being seen, they are present with you."
– **St. Francis de Sales**

At the time Francis de Sales became provost of the Diocese of Geneva, the area was a hotbed of Calvinism, and Francis aimed to bring as many of them back to the Church as he could. He went door to door trying to get Calvinists to speak with him, but all too often the door remained closed or was slammed in his face. He began writing out his explanations of Catholic doctrine and slipping them under doors, which was among the first known uses of religious tracts to communicate the Catholic faith to those who had left or fallen away from it. In addition to many such pamphlets, Francis wrote two well-regarded books and is known today as the patron saint of the Catholic press.

"Consider the pains which martyrs have endured, and think how even now many people are bearing afflictions beyond all measure greater than yours, and say, 'Of a truth my trouble is comfort, my torments are but roses as compared to those whose life is a continual death, without solace, or aid or consolation, borne down with a weight of grief tenfold greater than mine.'"
– **St. Francis de Sales**

Francis de Sales was a kind, humble, and gentle man who was very successful in bringing souls into the Church, or back to it. While serving as provost of the Diocese of Geneva, he set himself the challenges of bringing 60,000 Calvinists back into the fold. He reached out to people who wouldn't open the door to him through their children, letting parents see his kindness and patience as he played with their young ones. During the three years he spent going door to door in Calvinist areas he brought 40,000 people into the Church, largely by adhering to the axiom he lived by: "A spoonful of honey attracts more flies than a barrelful of vinegar."

> "A man makes the most progress and merits the most grace precisely in those matters wherein he gains the greatest victories over self and most mortifies his will."
> **– St. Francis de Sales**

Even after becoming bishop of Geneva in 1602, Francis de Sales continued to perform such priestly duties as hearing confessions and teaching catechism classes. He was the model of humility and good-natured kindness—so much so that nobody realized he had worked hard for more than two decades to gain control over what he described as his quick temper. For that reason, he is sometimes referred to as the "Gentleman Saint." Interestingly, as bishop of Geneva, Francis was only in the city on two occasions, and on one of those he was simply passing through on his way elsewhere. He made his home in Annecy, France, about 22 miles south of Geneva.

"Obedience is a consecration of the heart, chastity of the body, and poverty of all worldly goods to the Love and Service of God. Blessed indeed are the obedient, for God will never permit them to go astray."
– **St. Francis de Sales**

In 1610, Francis de Sales co-founded the Order of Visitation of Mary with St. Jane de Chantal. It was initially not meant to be a religious order, but rather a congregation where the sisters would be cloistered only for the first year of their novitiate. They would subsequently go out into the community to visit the poor and sick. It was not a model that church officials felt comfortable with, and the archbishop began pressuring Francis to transform his congregation into a traditional religious order. He held out for a year before acceding in 1616. Francis insisted, however, that not only virgins could join, but also widows with no children to care for, the aged who were of sound mind, the crippled who were sound of mind and heart, and the sick whose diseases were not communicable.

"The Devil doesn't fear austerity but holy obedience."
– **St. Francis de Sales**

The concept of spiritual direction was the keystone of the relationship between Francis de Sales and his dear friend, St. Jane Frances de Chantal. They met in 1604, when Jane, a young widow, heard him preach in Dijon, France. She believed him to be the person she had seen in a vision and who had been sent to her by God to be her spiritual director. (Francis reported having also seen Jane in a vision before meeting her.) Spiritual direction is the process through which the Church guides the faithful to the attainment of eternal happiness, or Christian perfection. A confessor is, in this sense, also a director of conscience. The surviving letters from their correspondence provide perhaps the best-known example of spiritual direction.

> "All the science of the Saints is included in these two things: To do, and to suffer. And whoever had done these two things best, has made himself most saintly."
> – **St. Francis de Sales**

In the 17th century, true holiness was considered to be attainable only by the ordained and those in religious life. Lay people were not thought to be able to devote the necessary time to contemplation and prayer because they were actively involved in the world and did not have the luxury of withdrawing from it. Francis did not agree with this view. He believed that every Christian was called to holiness regardless of their immersion in earthly matters, a view that was closer to the teachings of Jesus and the lives of early Christians than the prevailing position of the Church during his own time. His goal in providing spiritual direction was to help those he advised become more Christ-like, just as it was the goal for his own ongoing spiritual development.

> "Stretch forth your hand towards God as an infant towards its father to be conducted by Him."
> – **St. Francis de Sales**

Just as Francis urged the faithful to reach out to God as an infant reaching for its father's hand, he also used the analogy of romantic love to describe the ideal relationship with God. He spoke of the intense desire to always be in the presence of one's beloved, to hold tight and never let go, to be obsessed with that one person. All of these, he maintained, should characterize one's love of God.

"You learn to speak by speaking, to study by studying, to run by running, to work by working, and just so, you learn to love by loving. All those who think to learn in any other way deceive themselves."
– **St. Francis de Sales**

To Francis de Sales, it was impossible to love God without loving God's children. We learn to love God by loving each other, without judgment. The corollary to this is being as gentle and forgiving with ourselves as we are with our neighbors. In the saint's words, "To be an angel in prayer and a beast in one's relations with people is to go lame on both legs."

"Many would be willing to have afflictions provided that they not be inconvenienced by them."
– **St. Francis de Sales**

In 1605, Bishop Francis was introduced to a young deaf-mute named Martin. In the 17th century, people who could neither hear nor speak were thought to be mentally impaired and not worth trying to educate, so Martin had never received any religious instruction. Determined that Martin learn about God's love, the bishop determined to teach him about the Catholic faith, which he accomplished by inventing his own sign language. Martin turned out to be intelligent and an apt pupil and was able to receive the Holy Eucharist in 1606 and was confirmed two years later. Bishop Francis hired Martin to be his gardener and served as Martin's confessor. Martin was devastated when Bishop Francis died and visited the grave nearly every day. He wasted away with grief and died within a few weeks of the Bishop's death. Consequently, St. Frances de Sales is the patron of catechists, the deaf, and the hearing-impaired.

> "If, when stung by slander or ill-nature, we wax proud and swell with anger, it is a proof that our gentleness and humility are unreal and mere artificial show."
> **– St. Francis de Sales**

Bishop Francis maintained a full schedule of work and travel even when his health began to fail. He was in more demand than ever, called upon for counsel by royalty and Church officials while continuing to preach and catechize and provide spiritual direction to many. In 1622, he was part of the Duke of Savoy's entourage for the Duke's Christmas tour in Avignon, France. During a stop in Lyon to visit a new Visitation convent, he exchanged what would turn out to be his last words with Mother Jane Francis de Chantal. She told him that she expected him to be canonized one day and that she hoped to take part in his canonization. On the day of his death, she was in Grenoble, deep in prayer, when she heard a voice say, "He is no more." She wasted no time in gathering his writings and other evidence to start the process of recommending him for canonization in which she played a key role.

> "Most emphatically I say it, if possible, fall out with no one, and on no pretext whatever suffer your heart to admit anger and passion. Saint James says, plainly and unreservedly, that 'the wrath of man worketh not the righteousness of God.'"
> – **St. Francis de Sales**

Bishop Francis remained in a guest house on the grounds of the Visitation convent in Lyon during the last month of his life in 1622. One of the sisters, aware of his rapidly declining health, begged him to pray for healing, but he refused. He assured her that Mother de Chantal and his good friend, Vincent de Paul, the Visitation order's new spiritual director, would be doing enough praying for him. As frail as he was, he preached and counseled the sisters though a busy Christmas season. He suffered a stroke on the day after Christmas, slipped in and out of consciousness, and on the Feast of Holy Innocents, December 28, he succumbed. The last word he spoke was "Jesus."

"Obedience is a virtue of so excellent a nature, that Our Lord was pleased to mark its observance upon the whole course of His life; thus He often says, He did not come to do His Own will, but that of His Heavenly Father."
– **St. Francis de Sales**

St. Francis de Sales was beatified in 1661, canonized in 1665, and proclaimed a Doctor of the Church in 1877. His heart is enshrined in the church of the Visitation in Lyon, France, where he died. His body was originally entombed near the high altar of the church of the first convent of the Visitation in Annecy but was removed during the French Revolution to prevent its desecration. It lies there again today in the Basilica of the Visitation in Annecy, France, next to the casket holding the remains of his dear friend, St. Jane de Chantal. The Basilica, built in the 1930s, features stained glass windows depicting events in the lives of both St. Francis de Sales and St. Jane de Chantal.

G

> "I will attempt day by day to break my will into pieces. I want to do God's Holy Will, not my own."
> – **St. Gabriel of Our Lady of Sorrows (St. Gabriel Possenti)**

Francis Possenti, born in Italy in 1838, was the eleventh of thirteen children. Two siblings and his mother died by the time he was four, and he would lose two more brothers by the time he was thirteen. Though Francis was known to be pious and charitable, he was also vain, short-tempered, and a ladies' man deeply involved in the social scene. Twice he narrowly escaped death, first from illness and then from a stray bullet. Each time he promised to enter religious life if he recovered, and each time he failed to keep his promise. The third time he made this promise, he recovered and actually made plans to join the Jesuits but didn't follow through. The end of a cholera epidemic that took the life of another sibling was marked by a procession of the icon of the Virgin Mary. As it passed him, he heard an inner voice asking why he was still alive. He entered the Passionist novitiate in Morrovalle in 1856, took the name Gabriel of Our Lady of Sorrows, and excelled in his studies. He soon started showing symptoms of tuberculosis but kept up his studies and spiritual formation, saying that he welcomed a slow death so he would have time to prepare spiritually. He was admired by his community for his devotion to the Virgin Mary. Gabriel died in 1862, before he could be ordained, and was canonized in 1920.

> "If you really want to love Jesus, first learn to suffer, because suffering teaches you to love."
> – **St. Gemma Galgani**

Through much of her brief life, Gemma Galgani, born in Italy in 1878, had mystical experiences including a remarkable relationship with her guardian angel. After her death, her spiritual director and biographer, Father Germano, would write, "Gemma saw her guardian angel with her own eyes, touched him with her hand, as if he were a being of this world, and would talk to him as would one friend to another." He appeared to her hovering in the air, with wings outstretched, and would also kneel with her in prayer. When she was ill, she saw him standing beside her bed, blessing her. He guided her in spiritual matters, corrected her behavior, and taught her how to act in the presence of God. She also sent him on "errands," carrying a question or request to Heaven for her, and he would return to her with a response. Gemma's guardian angel also delivered letters she wrote to her confessor, which she would leave beneath a shrine in the house where she was living because she had no money for postage and never knew where to find Father Germano on his travels. The unstamped letters unfailingly appeared wherever Father Germano was.

"Just as thoughts send out vibrations to which there is a creative and attractive power, gratitude stimulates the field of etheric energy that surrounds you on a subtle level to bring into your life more of what brings you joy."
– St. Genevieve

The exact date of St. Genevieve's birth is not known, but she is believed to have been in her late eighties when she died in Paris, France in 512. When St. Germain and St. Lupus were traveling through France on a mission to combat heresy, they stopped briefly in the village of Nanterres, just outside of Paris. St. Germain saw a little girl in the crowd that gathered around the travelers and instantly recognized her as having been chosen by God to carry out an important mission. He called the girl and her parents forward and told them that she would be an example that would inspire many to convert, and he asked Genevieve if she would remain pure and consecrate herself to Christ as His spouse. She said that was her greatest desire and asked for St. Germain's blessing, which he bestowed, along with a brass medal engraved with a cross. He told her to wear the medal always as a sign of her consecration to God and her devotion to Christ, and she did so for the remainder of her life.

> "Focusing upon the positive by counting your blessings, or using positive affirmations in the fertile time before you fall asleep is an invitation to both your subconscious mind and your pre-conscious mind to use your dreams as a way to show you insights, solutions and new creative ideas."
> **– St. Genevieve**

Having saved Paris on several occasions, St. Genevieve is the city's patron and protector. With the intervention of St. Germain, Genevieve convinced the citizens of Paris that the city would be spared the wrath of Attila the Hun and his hordes during their campaign to conquer Gaul, and when they were, she was acclaimed as the savior of Paris. A little more than 30 years later, when Paris was blockaded and under siege by Childeric, king of a Germanic tribe, Genevieve once again came to the aid of the starving population. She led an expedition of small boats that slipped past the blockade and back again with supplies gathered from neighboring villages. When the siege was over, Childeric, impressed by Genevieve's courage, granted her request to free the prisoners he was holding. After her death, Genevieve miraculously ended the epidemic that was sickening and killing people throughout France. The Bishop of Paris ordered her casket to be carried through the streets of the city, and according to reports of the day, thousands who saw or touched it were cured.

"Who except God can give you peace? Has the world ever been able to satisfy the heart?"
– **St. Gerard Majella**

Born into poverty in Muro, Italy in 1726, Gerard Majella trained as a sewing apprentice and became a servant in the household of the local bishop. He gave his earnings to his widowed mother, to the poor of Muro, and as offerings to the Church. He fasted for long periods and became so pale and thin that he was turned down twice by the Capuchin monastery because of poor health. At age 23 he joined the Congregation of the Most Holy Redeemer and became a professed lay brother. He died six years later and was canonized in 1904 by Pope St. Pius X for the miracles attributed to him.

> "The Most Blessed Sacrament is Christ made visible. The poor sick person is Christ again made visible."
> – **St. Gerard Majella**

St. Gerard Majella had the mystic abilities of levitation, bilocation, and reading souls. He performed several miracles during his lifetime. He cured with the sign of the cross a child who had fallen into boiling water and restored life to a boy who had fallen from a cliff. He got rid of the mice infesting a farmer's crop and caused a poor family's scant supply of wheat to last until the next harvest through simple blessings, and on several occasions, he caused bread to multiply for poor people. Shortly before his death in 1755 he performed the miracle for which he became the patron saint of pregnancy. Years earlier, he had dropped his handkerchief, which a young girl picked up and tried to return to him. He told her to keep it, telling her that she might need it someday. As a married woman, she went into labor prematurely and was in danger of losing the baby. When Gerard's handkerchief was applied to her body while prayers were said, her pains stopped, and she gave birth to a healthy baby.

O Sacred Heart of Jesus, fountain of eternal life, Your Heart is a glowing furnace of Love. You are my refuge and my sanctuary.
– **St. Gertrude the Great**

Gertrude was born in Germany in 1256 and is believed to have entered the Cistercian monastery school of Helfta in Saxony at the age of four, though the circumstances surrounding such an early enrollment are unknown. As a Benedictine nun, at the age of 25, Gertrude began having visions and would continue having them until the day she died. She regarded her first vision as a rebirth that changed her life forever, describing her former self as a "blind and insane woman." Gertrude is remembered as one of the great mystics of the 13th century. Hers was a form of nuptial mysticism, as she saw herself as the bride of Christ. She once had a vision in which she rested her head near the wound in Jesus' side and was able to hear his beating heart. Gertrude wrote prolifically, though many of her works have been lost. The second of the five books of *The Herald of Divine Love* includes her descriptions of her visions. Gertrude died in 1301 at the age of 46. She was never formally canonized but was declared a saint in 1677 by Pope Clement XII because of her veneration by her community.

> "Affliction strengthens the vigor of our soul, whereas happiness weakens it."
> **– Pope St. Gregory the Great**

Pope St. Gregory the Great never aspired to the papacy. In fact, he wanted nothing more than a monastic life, but he felt that he had no choice but to serve God in whatever capacity he was called to. He was born around 540 into a Rome that was but a vestige of the once powerful Western Roman Empire. Wealthy, aristocratic families still wielded great influence, however, and Gregory's father, Gordianus, was a senator and Prefect of Rome, until he retired and entered religious life. When he was 33, Gregory would also become Prefect of Rome, but after his father's death he converted the family's Roman villa into a monastery dedicated to St. Andrew and became a Benedictine monk in 574. He subsequently established six more monasteries on estates his family owned in Sicily.

> "There are in truth three states of the converted: the beginning, the middle, and the perfection. In the beginning, they experience the charms of sweetness; in the middle, the contests of temptation; and in the end, the fullness of perfection."
> **– Pope St. Gregory the Great**

Gregory counted his first three years of monastic life as the happiest period of his life, but it was also a life of rigorous discipline. He fasted for days at a time and deprived himself of sleep, and he expected the same austerity of his fellow monks. Upon returning to the monastery after a six-year absence, he was displeased to see that the monks had become worldlier and seemed have relaxed in ways that diminished the holiness of St. Andrew's. After a deathbed confession by one of the monks, Brother Justus, revealed that he had stolen three gold coins, Gregory ordered everyone to leave the man to die alone. He then ordered the monk's body and the three coins to be thrown onto the dung heap. Taking mercy on the man's soul, Gregory offered 30 masses for the confessed thief.

> "The greatness of contemplation can be given to none but those who love."
> **– Pope St. Gregory the Great**

During Gregory's time, Rome was threatened by the Germanic Lombards who practiced Arian Christianity. The Roman senate was nearly defunct, civil authority rested with the Byzantine emperor, and waves of deadly plagues and famine decimated the population. These were only some of the challenges facing Rome. Gregory wrote extensively of the depravities of the Lombards and the suffering they inflicted on the population of Rome. It was Gregory's desire to protect the people of Rome that led him to accept the Prefecture when what he craved was a life of quiet monasticism. Pope Pelagius II sent Gregory, as Prefect of Rome, to serve as permanent ambassador to the imperial court in Constantinople and ordered him to seek military assistance to defend Rome against the Lombards, but the request was denied. During the six years he spent in Constantinople, Gregory gained an understanding of the political situation in the East that would be of great value during his papacy.

> "The only true riches are those that make us rich in virtue. Therefore, if you want to be rich, beloved, love true riches. If you aspire to the heights of real honor, strive to reach the kingdom of Heaven. If you value rank and renown, hasten to be enrolled in the heavenly court of the Angels."
> **– Pope St. Gregory the Great**

Gregory was in the Roman Forum one day when a group of English slaves were being sold. When told that the tall, blond youths were Angles, he became determined that they should know God's grace. He bought them all and brought them to the monastery to be educated in the Catholic faith and baptized. In the process, he decided to seek permission from Pope Pelagius II to travel with some of his monks to England to convert the English people. Though he was granted permission, the people of Rome were so upset about him leaving that they demanded his recall. Three days after Gregory's party set off for England, papal messengers caught up with them and bore Gregory back to Rome in triumph, to the delight of the people of Rome. Later, as pope, Gregory sent forty monks from St. Andrew's, led by the Italian prior Augustine, to preach Catholicism to the English. Their success resulted in the canonization of Augustine of Canterbury and earned Gregory the title of Apostle to the English.

> "To do penance is to bewail the evil we have done, and to do no evil to bewail."
> – **Pope St. Gregory the Great**

When Pope Pelagius II was felled by plague during an epidemic that left bodies piled up in the streets of Rome, the people of Rome elected Gregory to succeed him. The prospect of leaving the monastery dismayed him, and he wrote to his friend, St. Leander, of his reluctance to assume the papacy: "The burden of this honor weighs me down." He wrote to Emperor Maurice asking him to void the election, but the letter was intercepted by the Roman Prefect who replaced it with his own letter begging the emperor to confirm the election without delay. In the interim, Gregory preached a sermon asking the people to gather together in a procession from each of the regions of Rome to the Basilica of the Blessed Virgin Mary, praying all the way for God to end the plague that was decimating the city. Eighty of the marchers fell dead of the plague before reaching the basilica.

"The proof of love is in the works. Where love exists, it works great things. But when it ceases to act, it ceases to exist."
– St. Gregory the Great

Gregory was the first monk to become pope, and he managed to retain his monastic spirit for the remainder of his life while providing both civil and religious leadership. During the 14 years of his pontificate, he was a zealous guardian of Catholic doctrine and made significant changes to the Mass. But he also saw to the practical needs of the people of Rome, many of whom were refugees forced to flee the advancing Lombards. With the Roman economy in ruins, Gregory set up a system of charitable relief for the poor and fed the hungry from his family's remaining estates in Sicily and from the vast land holdings of the Church. The wealthy families of Rome followed his example and donated generously in expiation of their sins. Beloved by the people, Gregory was canonized immediately by popular acclamation upon his death in 604 at the age of 64. He was later named a Doctor of the Church and one of the Latin Fathers.

To imitate our Lord's own humility, we must return to the simplicity of God's little ones."
– **St. Hilary of Poitiers**

Hilary was born and raised a pagan, but his search for meaning in life led him to the Scriptures where he found the answers he was seeking. He converted and was chosen by the people and clergy of Poitiers (in present-day France) to serve as bishop. Hilary lived during the time of the Arian controversy and was exiled to the East in 356 for failing to support their condemnation of St. Athanasius. While in exile, Hilary spent his time studying and writing. Released from exile after three years, he traveled through Greece and Italy on his way home, preaching against the Arians along the way. Back in Poitiers, he started writing hymns, as he'd seen how effectively the hymns of the East were used as pro-Arian propaganda. His were the first Western hymns that can be attributed to a known writer. Hilary died in 367 or 368 and was proclaimed a Doctor of the Church in 1851.

I

> "I have no taste for corruptible food nor for the pleasures of this life. I desire the bread of God, which is the flesh of Jesus Christ, who was of the seed of David; and for drink I desire his blood, which is love incorruptible."
> – **St. Ignatius of Antioch**

Ignatius was consecrated as the second Bishop of Antioch around 69 A.D. by the Apostle Peter. What is known about his life and works comes primarily from the seven letters he wrote to the Christians in the communities he passed through while being taken to Rome to face martyrdom during the reign of Emperor Trajan. Ignatius was a disciple of the Apostle John and was a staunch defender of the early Church. In the year 107 he was sentenced to be devoured by wild beasts in the Coliseum because of his refusal to renounce Christianity. The long journey under guard to Rome gave him ample opportunity to write his letters to encourage, instruct, and inspire Christians in the communities where they stopped throughout Asia Minor and Greece. Arriving in Rome on the last day of the games, Ignatius went without fear to his death and was killed immediately by two ravenous lions. St. Ignatius of Antioch was the first to refer to the community of Christians as the "Catholic Church," for the fact that it was open to anyone wanting to follow Jesus.

> "God gives each one of us sufficient grace ever to know His holy will, and to do it fully."
> – **St. Ignatius of Loyola**

St. Ignatius of Loyola didn't consider a religious life until he was about 30. He was born into a Spanish Basque family of minor nobility and grew up dreaming of glory on the battlefield, but that was not meant to be. Spain was at war with France, and in 1521, Ignatius was seriously wounded in a battle the Spanish troops were losing. He was carried home and underwent months of painful treatments and bed rest. He asked for something to read to take his mind of the pain and boredom. He expected tales of knighthood and courtly love, like *The Song of Roland* or *El Cid*, but he was given a book about the life of Jesus and a book of stories about saints. Until then, Ignatius hadn't been very devout. He believed in God and went to Mass, but as he read about the saints, he was fascinated by their deeds and their devotion to God. During the remainder of his recovery, he thought a lot about the good he could do in the world if he made use of the gifts God had given him. He prayed, and he thought about his life up to that point, and he felt that he was being called to God's service.

> "Few souls understand what God would accomplish in them if they were to abandon themselves unreservedly to Him and if they were to allow His grace to mold them accordingly."
> **– St. Ignatius of Loyola**

The book Ignatius had read about the life of Jesus had a profound effect on him because it describes a spiritual exercise that he found very helpful to him in discerning his calling and deciding to enter religious life. The exercise involved imagining oneself present during the major events in Christ's life. Ignatius found it so effective that he began devising his own spiritual exercises. He kept a diary of his own spiritual journey over the years, and he drew upon it in writing his book, *The Spiritual Exercises,* which earned him a reputation as an expert in spiritual direction.

> "The vigor with which you resist the enemy will be the measure of the reward which will follow the combat."
> **– St. Ignatius of Loyola**

When Ignatius was well enough to leave his sick room, he kept vigil for three days in Santa Maria de Montserrat, a Benedictine monastery, and then laid his sword in front of a ceramic tile depiction of the Black Madonna. He gave away everything else, shedding his old life and embarking on a new one dressed in a beggar's garb. He made a deal to work in a hospital in exchange for a place to sleep and relied on begging for food. He spent as much time as he could in an isolated cave where he could do his spiritual exercises without disturbance or distraction. During the ten months that he lived this way, Ignatius worked his way through his feelings and fears and gained an understanding of God's plan for him.

> "More determination is required to subdue the interior man than to mortify the body; and to break one's will than to break one's bones."
> – **St. Ignatius of Loyola**

Ignatius knew that to carry out what he believed to be his mission, converting non-believers to Catholicism, he would need a different kind of education than he'd received as a child. For one thing, Latin was the language of the Church, and he didn't know a word of it. So, he returned to Barcelona and, at 30, ended up learning Latin in a grammar school class of young children. Once he'd mastered Latin and some other basic classes, Ignatius moved on to study at universities and loved to talk about spiritual matters with others. It was inevitable that he would come to the attention of the Inquisition. He was accused of preaching without having the necessary training in theology, which could result in spreading misinformation or causing misunderstanding. That would be considered heresy. But after three different bouts of questioning by Inquisitors, Ignatius was always found innocent.

> "Teach us to give and not count the cost."
> – **St. Ignatius of Loyola**

At the age of 38, Ignatius enrolled in the College of St. Barbe of the University of Paris. He earned his master's degree when he was 44 and would have continued on for a doctorate, but he was rejected because he was considered too old. He shared quarters in Paris with Peter Faber and Frances Xavier. As their friendship grew, Ignatius shared his religious exercises with them. Word of their activities spread, and other men joined them. The group called themselves "Friends in the Lord." They had a common goal of going to the Holy Land to convert non-believers. Given the political and military situation at the time, the Friends in the Lord shifted their destination to Rome. When they presented themselves to the pope in 1540, Pope Paul III approved Ignatius and his friends as a religious order. The others convinced Ignatius to be their first leader, though he thought himself unworthy of the position. Thus, the Friends in the Lord became the Society of Jesus, known to many as Jesuits.

"Here is the difference between the joys of the world and the cross of Jesus Christ: after having tasted the first, one is disgusted with them; and on the contrary, the more one partakes of the cross, the greater the thirst for it."
– **St. Ignatius of Loyola**

Given that their first members came together as university students and their common interest in converting non-believers, it was only natural that the Society of Jesus would focus on education. They believed that education and reason were essential to fighting heresy and bringing people into the Church. The schools the order established employed a pedagogic model similar to the formal, highly structured model they were familiar with from their time at the College of St. Barbe of the University of Paris. Under Ignatius's leadership, the Society of Jesus established 35 schools.

"To use profitably for our neighbor's salvation the gifts nature has given us, they must be actuated from within and draw their strength there from."
– **St. Ignatius of Loyola**

During his long recuperation from his battle wounds, Ignatius had a vision of the Blessed Virgin holding baby Jesus. The intensity of his feelings at the sight of such purity filled him with disgust for the sins he committed during his youth and his military life. He knew that the strength of his aversion to the mere idea of his past sins of the flesh was proof that the vision had been sent by God to help him realize there was a purer love, the love between God and His children.

"Who could count all those who have had wealth, power, honor? But their glory, their riches were only lent to them, and they wore themselves out in preserving and increasing that which they were forced to abandon one day."
– St. Ignatius of Loyola

The Jesuit Constitutions that Ignatius wrote stressed absolute self-denial and obedience, which are consistent with his own sense of order and military discipline. Translated from the Latin, the motto established for the Order was "as if a dead body," meaning "as well-disciplined as a corpse." The Constitutions were adopted in 1553, three years before Ignatius would die in Rome. It was an order with no monasteries, as its members were meant to take action in the world, not cloister themselves away from the world.

"We should speak to God as a friend speaks to his friend, or a servant to his master, sometimes asking a favor, sometimes accusing ourselves of our faults, sometimes laying before Him all that concerns us, our thoughts, our doubts, our projects, and our dispositions, and asking counsel from Him in all these things."
– **St. Ignatius of Loyola**

When Ignatius and his group of Friends in the Lord were on the way to Rome to seek a mission from the Pope, they stopped at a small chapel. In the chapel, Ignatius had a vision of The Eternal Father and his Son, and heard the Father telling him He would be favorable to Ignatius and his followers in Rome. And then he heard the Father tell the Son to take Ignatius as his servant. Finally, he heard the Son speak to his heart, telling him that he wanted Ignatius himself to serve "us" – Father and Son.

"Go and set the whole world on fire with the fire of Divine love."
– **St. Ignatius of Loyola**

When Ignatius told his group in 1539 that they would carry out whatever mission the Pope gave them when they presented themselves to him in Rome, he warned that they could end up being scattered to distant lands. This is, in fact, what happened. At first Pope Paul II asked Ignatius to send six men to the East to convert non-believers, but when Ignatius pointed out that sending six would limit his ability to send anyone to the other areas where Calvinism was spreading, Francis Xavier, Ignatius's old roommate, was sent to India with another man, and it was the last the two friends would ever see of each other.

"Take it for a principle to concede readily in the beginning of a conversation with those whose aspirations are only earthly; but reserve yourself for the end and try to cover with a layer of gold the metal of their conversation, whatsoever it may be."
– **St. Ignatius of Loyola**

From 1547 until his death, Ignatius had a trusted private secretary, Juan Alfonso de Polanco, who helped him with his writing. Ignatius generated an enormous amount of correspondence, and as his health deteriorated, some of the burden of writing hundreds of letters to some of the most prominent personages of the time shifted to Juan. The secretary also helped Ignatius finish getting the *Spiritual Exercises* ready for publication. Its lasting popularity is the reason for St. Ignatius being made the patron saint of spiritual retreats.

"Place before your eyes as models for imitation, not the weak and cowardly, but the fervent and courageous."
– **St. Ignatius of Loyola**

In his later years, Ignatius suffered great pain from a variety of ailments, including gallstones and problems with his liver, and he was often confined to bed. On more than one occasion during the last five or six years of his life, he was thought to be dying, and he grew progressively weaker and frailer. In July of 1556, he was taken to a farm in the countryside to see if he would benefit from the fresh air, but within a couple of weeks he was moved back to La Strada, and he died there four days later. The immediate cause of death was malaria, which broke out in Rome periodically and was referred to as the Roman Fever. Ignatius died as dawn was breaking, before he could be given the last rites. At the time of his death, the Society of Jesus had more than a thousand members.

"Before choosing, let us examine well whether the attachment we feel for an object springs solely from the love of God."
– **St. Ignatius of Loyola**

Ignatius believed that the way to convert non-believers was to connect with them through something that is familiar and comfortable to them. One of his conversions came about through a game of billiards. A French Doctor of Theology challenged him to a game. Ignatius accepted the challenge on the condition that if the doctor won, Ignatius would be his servant for a month and do whatever the doctor asked of him. But if Ignatius won, the doctor would have to do only one thing for him. It was a daring bet for Ignatius, who knew nothing about billiards. Still, Ignatius did win, and he asked only one thing of the doctor—that he complete the *Spiritual Exercises*. It took the doctor a month to do so, and through the process, he became a convert.

"Truth always ends by victory; it is not unassailable, but invincible."
 – St. Ignatius of Loyola

Ignatius was placed in a small wooden shrine which was buried in the Maria della Strada Church that had been his base in Rome. Two years later that church was demolished and replaced with the larger Church of the Gesu, where Ignatius was reinterred. Beatified in 1609 and canonized in 1622, St. Ignatius of Loyola is the patron of Catholic soldiers, the Basque Country, the Society of Jesus, soldiers, educators and education, the Military Ordinate of the Philippines, and several dioceses and municipalities.

"My confidence is placed in God who does not need our help for accomplishing his designs. Our single endeavor should be to give ourselves to the work and to be faithful to him, and not to spoil his work by our shortcomings."
– **St. Isaac Jogues**

French-born Jesuit missionary Isaac Jogues arrived in Quebec, Canada in 1636 and spent the next six years working with other missionaries to convert the Huron Indians around the Great Lakes. In 1642 he led an expedition to Quebec to obtain supplies. On the way back to the mission, the party was ambushed and captured by a band of Iroquois, enemies of the Hurons. The captives were tortured, and Isaac's assistant, Rene Goupil, and their Christian converts were killed. Isaac spent thirteen months as a slave of the Iroquois until, aided by Dutch Calvinists, he escaped and returned to France. Received with great honors at court, he was named a martyr by Pope Urban VII because of the torture he had suffered, which included the mutilation of his hands. (Several of his fingers had been bitten off.) Within a few months, Isaac returned to negotiate peace with his former captors, resulting in a treaty. He went back to Quebec but after a brief stay once more sought out the Iroquois with the goal of converting them. While he was in Quebec, however, illness and crop failure had turned the Iroquois against the missionaries. Once again, he was captured, but this time he was martyred by decapitation. St. Isaac Jogues was canonized in 1930 with seven other North American martyrs, including St. Rene Goupil.

> "Prayer purifies us, reading instructs us... If a man wants to be always in God's company, he must pray regularly and read regularly. When we pray, we talk to God; when we read, God talks to us."
> **– St. Isidore of Seville**

St. Isidore of Seville lived in a time when the legacies of the Roman Empire were in danger of disappearing in a Spain that had been controlled by Goths for nearly 200 years. The modern world is indebted to him for preserving much knowledge that might otherwise have been lost to us over the intervening centuries. Isidore, regarded as the most learned man of his age, devoted the last years of his life to creating an encyclopedia of all existing knowledge, which he called *Etymologiae* and is sometimes referred to as *Origins*. He acted more as compiler and curator than as author, pulling together material, both ancient and modern, from 154 different authors, both Christian and pagan. St. Isidore's encyclopedia served as a textbook for nine centuries! It solidified his standing as the last of the great Latin Fathers of the Church. The encyclopedia was the capstone to a life devoted largely to bringing together the disparate cultural influences of the time into a blended Spanish civilization.

> "Do not permit yourself to be a spectacle for the gossip of others; do not allow your honor to be degraded. Do not associate with vain people. Avoid the bad; rebuff the indolent. Flee overmuch association with men, especially those who are more inclined to vice."
> **– St. Isidore of Seville**

Isidore's much older brother, Leander, took charge of young Isidore's education. His methods were very harsh, but Isidore persisted and retained his love of learning, eventually becoming known as Spain's greatest educator. He established seminaries throughout Spain, wrote textbooks on a wide variety of subjects, and succeeded his brother Leander as bishop of Seville, a position Isidore would hold for 37 years. (Another brother, Fulgentius, was also a bishop, and his sister Florentina was an abbess. All three are revered as saints in Spain.) Isidore also developed a model for representative government and helped convert the Visigoths to Catholicism. One of the last things he did as he was dying in 636 at 76 years of age was to give everything he owned to the poor. He was canonized in 1598 by Pope Clement VIII and is regarded as the last of the Doctors of the Church.

> "If any of you lacks wisdom, let him ask God, who gives to all men generously and without reproaching, and it will be given him."
> **– St. James the Greater** (James 1:5)

James and his brother John, sons of Zebedee, were the second pair of brothers (also fishermen) to become disciples of Jesus. James, his brother John, and Simon Peter were the inner circle most favored by Jesus and privileged to witness events not seen by the other disciples: the raising of the daughter of Jairus from the dead, the agony of Jesus in the Garden of Gethsemane, and the transfiguration. James is believed to have been the first of the apostles to be martyred, because his is the only martyrdom of an apostle to appear in the New Testament. His beheading by sword was ordered by King Herod during the persecution of early Christians, most likely in the year 44. He is sometimes called St. James the Greater to distinguish him from the other disciple named James, who is referred to as James the Lesser because he was either shorter or younger. He is the patron of pilgrims and Spain. The Camino de Santiago (Way of St. James) is a network of pilgrim routes that have been in use for centuries and lead to the tomb of St. James in Santiago de Compostela in northwestern Spain. More than 278,000 people completed the pilgrimage in 2016.

> "The great method of prayer is to have none. If in going to prayer one can form in oneself a pure capacity for receiving the spirit of God, that will suffice for all method."
> **– St. Jane Frances de Chantal**

Jane Frances was raised by her father, president of the parliament of Burgundy, after the death of her mother when Jane was not yet two years old. One of the first things she did after marrying the Count de Chantal was to restore the practice of daily Mass in the castle. She was known as a devout and charitable woman, and she maintained those qualities in times of great trials and sorrow. The loss of three children in infancy and the death of her beloved husband when she was 28 tested her strength, but she sought spiritual direction from St. Francis de Sales, who encouraged her charitable works and remained her friend until his death. They worked together to establish the congregation of the Visitation of Holy Mary, or the Visitation Order, with an initial congregation of only three women. There were 86 Visitation houses by the time of Jane's death and 164 when she was canonized herself in 1767, 126 years after her death at the age of 69.

> "Hold your eyes on God and leave the doing to him. That is all the doing you have to worry about."
> – **St. Jane Frances de Chantal**

St. Vincent DePaul became Jane's new spiritual director when St. Francis de Sales had to return to Geneva. Jane suffered several personal losses during the years following the death of St. Francis de Sales in 1622, including the battlefield death of her son and the deaths of her son-in-law and friends when plague broke out in France in 1632. St. Vincent de Paul described Jane in these words: "While apparently enjoying the peace and easiness of mind of souls who have reached a high state of virtue, she suffered such interior trials that she often told me her mind was so filled with all sorts of temptations and abominations that she had to strive not to look within herself. But for all that suffering her face never lost its serenity, nor did she once relax in the fidelity God asked of her. And so, I regard her as one of the holiest souls I have ever met on this earth." St. Jane de Chantal is the patron of forgotten people, in-law problems, loss of parents, parents separated from children, and widows.

"You either belong wholly to the world or wholly to God."
– **St. Jean-Baptiste-Marie Vianney**

Jean-Baptiste-Marie Vianney grew up during the French Revolution, which started when he was a toddler and didn't end until he was thirteen. His life and worldview were shaped not only by his Catholic upbringing but also by the turmoil and reign of terror he witnessed as an impressionable child. Until it became too dangerous, the Vianney family traveled to remote farms where priests in hiding would conduct Mass. His first catechism teachers were two nuns whose communities had been dissolved yet were willing to instruct him in private. Young Jean, or John in English, developed a great admiration for the priests and other religious people who risked their lives by continuing their work in secret during the anticlerical phase of the revolution. He considered them heroes.

"What? The cross make us lose our inward peace? Surely it is the cross that bestows it on our hearts. All our miseries come from our not loving it."
– **St. Jean-Baptiste-Marie Vianney**

At the age of 20, John enrolled in the presbytery school in Écully, operated by the Abbe Balley, where he had to work very hard to make up for the years of education he'd missed out on during the revolution. The Catholic Church had been officially re-established a few years earlier, and John, an ecclesiastical student, should have been exempt from military service. However, Napoleon Bonaparte rescinded the exemption in dioceses where he needed to recruit more troops, and John was drafted in 1809.

"Sin is the executioner of the good God, and the assassin of the soul. It snatches us away from Heaven to precipitate us into Hell. And we love it! What folly! If we thought seriously about it, we should have such a lively horror of sin that we could not commit it."
– **St. Jean-Baptiste-Marie Vianney**

Illness cast John into the role of deserter when he didn't return to military duty upon his release from the hospital. Instead, he stopped to pray in a church and met a young man who offered to help him catch up with the troops but instead led John into the mountains, where several deserters were in hiding. He would live in a sympathetic widow's barn for the next 14 months under the name Jerome Vincent, hiding every time the gendarmes came through looking for deserters. During his stay there, he started a school in a nearby village under his assumed name.

"We ought to run after crosses as the miser runs after money. . . Nothing but crosses will reassure us at the Day of Judgment When that day shall come, we shall be happy in our misfortunes, proud of our humiliations, and rich in our sacrifices!"
– **St. Jean-Baptiste-Marie Vianney**

When deserters were granted amnesty in 1810, John returned to finish his studies in Écully then attended seminary. His academic performance was not up to par, and it looked doubtful that he would be ordained. However, it was argued that his piety outweighed his ignorance, and he was ordained a deacon in 1815. Following in the footsteps of the priests he so admired as a child, he was ordained a priest and was assigned to assist Abbe Balley at Écully. Three years later, after Balley's death, John became parish priest in the Ars parish, a town so small and insignificant that he had trouble finding it. One of his accomplishments was establishing a home for girls, called La Providence.

> "See, my children, a person who is in a state of sin is always sad. Whatever he does, he is weary and disgusted with every thing; while he who is at peace with God is always happy, always joyous. . . Oh, beautiful life! Oh, beautiful death!"
> **– St. Jean-Baptiste-Marie Vianney**

Father Vianney was disturbed by the religious ignorance and indifference that were the legacy of the French Revolution. He found it intolerable that many people spent the Sabbath working, drinking, or dancing rather than worshipping. He spent long hours trying to turn the people of his parish from blasphemy and refused to absolve anyone who would not give up dancing. Many welcomed his efforts, and as his fame spread, thousands of people every year traveled to hear him preach.

> "If someone said to you, 'I would like to become rich; what must I do?' you would answer him, 'You must labor.' Well, in order to get to Heaven, we must suffer."
> – **St. Jean-Baptiste-Marie Vianney**

One of the times that Father Vianney is said to have miraculously multiplied food occurred when the orphanage staff told him there was no food left to eat. The attic where corn was kept was completely empty. He bowed his head in prayer and then instructed one of the staff to go upstairs and fetch some corn. She came back empty-handed because she had been unable to open the attic door. When the door was forced open, they found that the attic was filled with corn from floor to ceiling.

> "The first thing about the angels that we ought to imitate is their consciousness of the Presence of God."
> **– St. Jean-Baptiste-Marie Vianney**

Father Vianney had a special devotion to St. Philomena since the tomb of the 15-year old martyr was discovered when he was only a year older than she was when she died. His relationship with St. Philomena has been described as a personal, supernatural friendship. In his position as parish priest in Ars, France, Father Vianney built an altar to her and installed the relic in it. When people came to him asking to be cured of their afflictions, he told them to appeal to St. Philomena for intercession with God, not to him. He assured them that St. Philomena had never disappointed him and had, in fact, cured him of a lethal illness. He routinely told those seeking a cure, especially a physical cure, to challenge her to prove that she could deliver one. For example, he told a woman whose left arm was paralyzed to say to St. Philomena, "Restore my arm to me or give me your own!" She experienced an immediate healing, as did many others who were instructed to challenge St. Philomena in this manner.

"The Devil writes down our sins - our Guardian Angel all our merits. Labor that the Guardian Angel's book may be full, and the Devil's empty."
– **St. Jean-Baptiste-Marie Vianney**

Father Vianney did not like it when the healed and their loved ones attributed cures to him rather than to St. Philomena. He reportedly made a deal with St. Philomena that when people came to him to be cured of a physical affliction, he would send them to her altar with the understanding that she would not heal their bodies until nine days later, when they were back home and would not associate their healing with the parish priest back in Ars. Nonetheless, Father Vianney himself is known to have brought about many healings.

"The happiness of man on earth, my children, is to be very good; those who are very good bless the good God, they love Him, they glorify Him, and do all their works with joy and love, because they know that we are in this world for no other end than to serve and love the good God."
– **St. Jean-Baptiste-Marie Vianney**

Father Vianney was concerned that the town of Ars would become so famous as a place for physical healing that people would forget about the potential for spiritual healing. He considered every conversion a miracle. He often attached conditions to a physical cure that required a corresponding attention to the person's soul. Two examples are commonly cited—telling a young, unchaste epileptic, "That is not the way to behave for one who desires to be cured," and telling a girl that the cure for her paralysis was contingent upon her becoming respectful of her mother. He also told people that curing a physical affliction might not be good for their soul, saying that "The greatest cross is having no cross."

"So, you will ask me, who then are the people most tempted? They are these, my friends; note them carefully. The people most tempted are those who are ready, with the grace of God, to sacrifice everything for the salvation of their poor souls, who renounce all those things which most people eagerly seek. It is not one devil only who tempts them, but millions seek to entrap them."
– **St. Jean-Baptiste-Marie Vianney**

As he grew older, Father Vianney craved a more contemplative life than was possible while serving the residents of Ars and the thousands of pilgrims arriving there every year in search of spiritual or physical healing. On four occasions, he attempted to leave Ars and enter a monastery, but it never worked out. He eventually abandoned the idea. He died in 1859 at age 73. Over 6,000 people, including 300 priests, were present at the funeral of the simple parish priest. He was beatified in 1905 and canonized in 1925. He is the patron saint of parish priests.

> "Be at peace with your own soul, then heaven and earth will be at peace with you."
> **– St. Jerome**

St. Jerome was born Eusebius Sophronius Hieronymus in 342 AD, in today's Croatia or Slovenia. Although the details of his early life are largely unknown, it's likely that his family was of some wealth and social standing. He was well-tutored in Latin and Greek and was regarded as headstrong and impulsive. He completed his education in Rome, where he spent his free time in the pursuit of pleasure, especially pleasures of the flesh, though he knew his behavior was immoral. The pangs of guilt he suffered led him to visit the crypts where he could easily imagine himself in the depths of Hell. But guilt alone wasn't enough to make Jerome mend his ways.

"One may understand by the nourishment of the swine the false philosophy of the world, the vain eloquence of oratory. Their cadence and harmony, in flattering the ear, possess the mind, and enchant the heart; but after one has read works of this kind with great attention, nothing is left but vacancy and confusion. Let us not delude ourselves by saying we do not put any faith in the fable, with which these authors have filled their writings. This reason does not justify us, since we scandalize others who think we approve of what they see us read."
– St. Jerome

While studying in Rome, Jerome practiced his Latin and Greek by transcribing the inscriptions on the tombs in the catacombs. He traveled quite a bit after completing his education, translating and copying books with the goal of building a personal library collection. In 374 in Antioch, he began writing his first work, *Concerning the Seven Beatings*. He also experienced the loss of several companions who sickened and died, though it's not clear whether they all had the same disease. Jerome also became ill and had a vision that intensified his religious feelings and changed the course of his life. He saw himself standing in judgment in front of Christ and being found wanting for having given to much attention to secular studies and interests. He spent the next four years praying and fasting while living as a hermit in the desert southwest of Antioch, where he continued to experience visions and bouts of illness.

> "When we pray we speak to God; but when we read, God speaks to us."
> **– St. Jerome**

Jerome had great mastery of Latin and Greek but was ignorant of Hebrew. He determined to learn the language as a way of exercising his faithfulness. Jerome found learning Hebrew to be a difficult and painful process, even with the help of a fellow monk who was a convert from Judaism, but he persisted. St. Jerome is perhaps best known today for his translation of the Scriptures from Hebrew and Old Latin. It was a task that occupied years of his life.

"In God's Name, the counsel of My Lord is safer and wiser than yours. You thought to deceive me, and it is yourselves who are deceived, for I bring you better succor than has ever come to any general or town whatsoever the succor of the King of Heaven. This succor does not come from me, but from God Himself, Who, at the prayers of Saint Louis and Saint Charlemagne, has had compassion on the town of Orleans, and will not suffer the enemy to hold at the same time the Duke and his town!"
– **St. Joan of Arc**

There are few saints whose story is as familiar to the public as that of Joan of Arc, patron saint of soldiers and of France. It captured the imaginations of writers including William Shakespeare, George Bernard Shaw, Mark Twain, and Bertholt Brecht. It's been translated into musical works, including a Rossini cantata and operas by Verdi and Tchaikovsky, interpreted in modern dance by Martha Graham, and depicted in art found in museums around the world. Condemned unjustly by an English court to burn at the stake for heresy, she was martyred in 1431, her eyes fixed on a cross held before her at her request, a small cross fashioned by an English soldier tucked insider her dress. Twenty-one years later, a posthumous retrial (the nullification trial) requested by Joan's mother and the Inquisitor General and authorized by the Pope found that Joan's original trial was unjust. It took the appellate court another four years to formally declare Joan innocent, in 1456.

> "Since God had commanded it, it was necessary that I do it. Since God commanded it, even if I had a hundred fathers and mothers, even if I had been a King's daughter, I would have gone nevertheless."
> **– St. Joan of Arc**

The charge of heresy leveled against Joan stemmed from disbelief that Joan's actions were commanded by the voices of St. Michael, St. Catherine, and St. Margaret, which Joan claimed she had been hearing from a very young age. For several years she had only heard them, but when she was 13, Saints Michael, Catherine, and Margaret appeared to her in a vision. This time they gave her specific instructions to drive the English out of France and to bring the dauphin to Reims to be crowned. Joan was 16 by the time she was able to present herself to the dauphin (later crowned King Henry VII of France) to offer her aid. His advisors feared that the voices Joan heard were of demonic origin, which would make her guilty of witchcraft, and they could not allow the dauphin's cause to be tainted by any hint of heresy. After checking into her background and interrogating Joan, a commission of inquiry found her beyond reproach, a good Christian of "humility, honesty, and simplicity." Theologians, however, while admitting that her mission was probably divinely inspired, insisted that she be tested to eliminate any doubt. The test was to lift the siege of Orleans, which Joan had claimed she would do. And that's exactly what she did. Defeating the French at Orleans convinced the theologians and the dauphin to let her continue her mission to rid France of the English.

> "About Jesus Christ and the Church, I simply know they're just one thing."
> – **St. Joan of Arc**

The Burgundians who were allied with the English captured Joan and held her for ransom before selling her to the English, who tried her as a witch and heretic in a trial that violated standard legal procedures of the time. The clerical notary charged with gathering evidence against Joan found none, but the trial proceeded anyway. Joan was denied legal counsel, and the tribunal consisted of pro-English clergy even though the Church's normal process required impartial clerics to be included. The Vice-Inquisitor of Northern France agreed to cooperate only after the English threatened his life. Joan was not held in an ecclesiastical prison guarded by nuns, which was the norm for prisoners of the Inquisition, but rather in a secular prison guarded by English soldiers. After fighting off an attempted rape, Joan wore men's clothing, which afforded more protection against sexual assault but also resulted in an added charge of heresy for cross-dressing.

> "One life is all we have, and we live it as we believe in living it. But to sacrifice what you are and to live without belief, that is a fate more terrible than dying."
> – **St. Joan of Arc**

One of the most illuminating exchanges during Joan's trial came when Joan was asked if she knew she was in God's grace. Joan, a simple, ill-educated peasant girl, would have had no way of knowing the question was a trap intended to elicit a response that would prove her guilt. Church doctrine was that there is no certainty, for anyone, of being in God's grace. So, answering "yes" would have violated doctrine and been an act of heresy. Answering "no" would have been a confession of guilt. Joan's interrogators were stunned when she evaded the trap by answering, "If I am not, may God put me there; and if I am, may God so keep me." Nevertheless, Joan was convicted of heresy and sentenced to death.

> "We should have frequent recourse to prayer and persevere a long time in it. God wishes to be solicited. He is not weary of hearing us. The treasure of His graces is infinite. We can do nothing more pleasing to him than to beg incessantly that He bestow them upon us."
> – **St. John Baptist de la Salle**

St. John Baptist de la Salle is best known as an educational reformer. He founded a community of teachers that became the Institute of the Brothers of the Christian Schools and established teachers' colleges in Rheims, Paris, and Saint-Denis in his native France. Born into a noble family in Rheims in 1651 and ordained in 1678, he dedicated his life to creating educational opportunities for the poor. He is regarded as the founder of the first Catholic schools and implemented important changes in the way both children and teachers were educated. For example, he felt strongly that teaching should be done in the common language spoken by students rather than in Latin, which was the language of the wealthy and of clergy. He also emphasized classroom teaching over the individual instruction that was common at the time. The schools he founded employed lay teachers as well as clerics, divided students into ability-based groups, and even offered Sunday classes for students who worked during the week. Many of his innovations are still reflected in modern education. Canonized in 1900, 181 years after his death, St. John Baptist de la Salle was named patron of teachers in 1950.

"When I see the devil has stopped ensnaring souls, I too will cease looking for new ways to save them from his wily deceits."
– **St. John Bosco**

Born Giovanni Melchiorre Bosco and known as Don Bosco, John Bosco was born in 1815, in a region of Italy recently ravaged by the Napoleonic Wars and suffering from drought and famine. Raised from the age of two by his widowed mother, he was very devout even as a young boy, influenced no doubt by her example of charity to the homeless despite her own poverty. He was also influenced throughout his life by a series of vivid dreams he had at the age of nine. In his dreams he saw many boys swearing as they played under the watchful eyes of a majestic man and woman who gave him advice he would never forget—that in meekness and charity he would "conquer these, your friends" and that if he remained strong, humble, and robust he would eventually understand everything. He then saw the boys turn into a pack of snarling beasts before the woman, who, with a wave of her hand, changed them into a peaceful flock of lambs.

"What I recommend most earnestly is not to lose heart when you are tempted. Do you wish to succeed? The best way is to reveal the temptations to your spiritual director immediately. The devil loves darkness. He always operates in the dark because he knows that if he is discovered he is beaten."
– **St. John Bosco**

As a boy, John was intrigued by magic and thought it was a good way to hold the attention of others. He learned some magic tricks and one Sunday evening, performed them for a group of his friends, and then recited for them the homily he had heard at Mass that day. His friends not only listened to the homily, but also prayed with John. John put on such shows regularly, and through them he recognized his calling to the priesthood. Throughout his life, John Bosco used what has become known as "gospel magic" to attract and engage the youth that were the focus of his mission. In 2002, nearly 70 years after his canonization, John was named as the patron of stage magicians.

"Do you want to outwit the devil? Never let him catch you idle. Work, study, pray, and you will surely overcome your spiritual enemy."
– **St. John Bosco**

John knew that he would need an education to become a priest, but his family's poverty was an obstacle. When he did find a priest who was willing to teach him, John's older brother was enraged and gave John a whipping because his help was needed on the family farm. So, John left home at the age of 12 and worked in a vineyard for two years until he found a priest, Joseph Cafasso (now a saint himself), who would help him prepare for seminary, which he entered at the age of 20. He was ordained six years later. During his first assignment, in the slums of Turin, Father Bosco worked with children living in poverty and became determined to keep them from ending up incarcerated like the many teenage boys he saw during his prison visits. He found them jobs and homes, assisted by his mother, who became known as Mamma Margherita. His own experiences with poverty and lack of opportunity undoubtedly helped fuel his passion for his work.

> "Ask your angel to console and assist you in your last moments."
> – **St. John Bosco**

Father Bosco worked tirelessly to improve the lives of young apprentices, who were often abused by their employers and forced to work long hours and do unpaid menial tasks not related to their apprenticeship. He worked with employers to negotiate contracts that gave apprentices the right to feast days off and banned beatings and other unfair and abusive practices. He also encouraged boys promising to consider religious life and helped prepare those who felt a call to the priesthood. Because of these activities, Father Bosco became a somewhat controversial figure, opposed by some parish priests who resented his work with street youth and accused him of stealing boys from parish churches. Turin's police chief thought that his practice of preaching and providing religious instruction in the streets was politically subversive. Father Bosco was undeterred by such opposition.

"When tempted, invoke your Angel. He is more eager to help you than you are to be helped! Ignore the devil and do not be afraid of him: He trembles and flees at the sight of your Guardian Angel."
– St. John Bosco

Father Bosco's life as an educator began with one boy who wandered in from the street to warm himself in the church while Father Bosco was preparing for Mass. He stopped the sacristan from throwing the boy out and struck up a conversation with the youth. He learned that he was an orphaned 16-year old bricklayer named Bartholomew. Father Bosco asked him to stay for Mass, and after Mass he invited Bartholomew to come back the following Sunday with his friends. That next Sunday four young boys came needing a hot meal and warm clothing, and the following week there were even more. Their numbers continued to increase, and the group became the first students in Father Bosco's wandering Oratory, meeting in public wherever they found space.

"Fly from bad companions as from the bite of a poisonous snake. If you keep good companions, I can assure you that you will one day rejoice with the blessed in Heaven; whereas if you keep with those who are bad, you will become bad yourself, and you will be in danger of losing your soul."
– **St. John Bosco**

In 1859, Father Bosco organized a group of seminarians and one teenage boy and established the Society of St. Francis de Sales, known commonly as the Salesians. Its mission was the same one he's been pursuing since he first started working with youth—helping them to stay out of trouble and grow spiritually. The many Salesian schools in operation today, whether in a remote African village or a bustling American city, operate with the philosophy that each school is not only a school, but also a house, a church, and a playground. Loving kindness, reason, and religion are the cornerstones of a Salesian education. There are Salesian schools in 124 nations, including non-Christian countries.

> "Never read books you aren't sure about... even supposing that these bad books are very well written from a literary point of view. Let me ask you this: Would you drink something you knew was poisoned just because it was offered to you in a golden cup?"
> **– St. John Bosco**

Father Bosco is reported to have performed several miraculous healings during his lifetime. Hundreds of people witnessed one that occurred on the feast of the Holy Cross in 1867, when an elderly woman, unable to walk unassisted asked for a blessing. Father Bosco told her to kneel, which she had not been able to do in many years. He took her crutches from her and she knelt easily for his blessing, weeping with joy. In 1877 a woman brought her 10-year old daughter to see Father Bosco on the eve of the feast of Mary Help of Christians. She told him that her daughter had been paralyzed on her right side and unable to speak for more than a month. He blessed her and asked her to make the sign of the cross. When she did so with her left hand, he told her to do it with her right hand, and she was able to, right arm no longer paralyzed. He then asked her to repeat some words after him, and she was no longer mute. And Father Bosco's former pupil and biographer told of Father Bosco raising a boy who had recently died. There are numerous accounts of other miracles performed by Father Bosco during his lifetime, as well as many attributed to the intercession of St. John Bosco.

> "Avoid slander because it is difficult to retract. Avoid offending anyone for to ask forgiveness is not delightful."
> – **St. John Cantius**

Pope John Paul II had an abiding devotion to this saint, John Cantius, born in 1390 in the tiny town of Kenty (sometimes spelled Kanti or Kanty), only a few miles from his own birthplace in southern Poland. Aside from a few years as a parish priest, Cantius spent his entire life in Krakow, where he had been educated and ordained. He taught in the Philosophy Department at the Jagiellonian University before becoming Director of the Theology Department. He was well known for his generosity and compassion and his efforts on behalf of the poor. Shortly after his death, he began to be credited for miracles achieved through his intercession, and before long, pilgrims were coming from all over Europe to his tomb in the university's church. St. John Cantius was canonized in 1676 and declared patron of Poland and Lithuania in 1737. When Pope John Paul II made his 1997 pilgrimage to Poland, he made it a point to pray at the tomb of the saint he'd admired for so long.

"The memory of insults is the residue of anger. It keeps sins alive, hates justice, ruins virtue, poisons the heart, rots the mind, defeats concentration, paralyzes prayer, puts love at a distance, and is a nail driven into the soul. If anyone has appeased his anger, he has already suppressed the memory of insults, while as long as the mother is alive the son persists. In order to appease the anger, love is necessary."
– **St. John Climacus**

Very little is known about the history of St. John Climacus (also known as John the Ladder, John Scholasticus, and John Sinaites), including exactly when he lived, which scholars now place in the seventh century. He was probably either Syrian or Palestinian, and he lived for about 20 years as a hermit at the foot of Mount Sinai. During those years he studied the lives of the saints and the Scriptures, becoming one of the most learned scholars of his time. At the age of 75 he accepted the invitation of the monks at Sinai to become their abbot. His reputation for wisdom spread, and he even received an unsolicited donation from Pope Gregory the Great for the hospital of Sinai, where pilgrims found lodging.

"Humility is the only thing that no devil can imitate."
– **St. John Climacus**

St. John Climacus is best known for the literary work, *The Climax*, from which his name was derived. The book is also known as *The Ladder of Perfection*, giving rise to the name John the Ladder. (John Sinaites comes from his association with Mount Sinai.) In writing it, John used the analogy of Jacob's Ladder, with 30 steps, each representing a year in Christ's life up to the point that He began His earthly ministry. The steps were organized in groups representing: the virtues necessary for an ascetic life (steps 1-7); instructions for overcoming vices and developing those virtues (steps 8-26); and the higher virtues that are attainable by leading an ascetic life (steps 27-30).

"Detachment is a withdrawal from all evil desires."
– **St. John Climacus**

The monk who would become a saint was convinced of the value of asceticism and monasticism in achieving spiritual growth and developing the highest of virtues: prayer, stillness, dispassion, and love. He was never more fulfilled than when he was living an eremitic life. John's treatise on aiming for Christian perfection through the monastic life was originally written for a specific, private audience—the abbot of a neighboring monastery—but it was widely read in both the East and the West. St. John Climacus is revered as a saint by the Roman Catholic Church, but he was never canonized.

"If a man wishes to be sure of the road he treads on, he must close his eyes and walk in the dark."
– **St. John of the Cross**

Juan de Yepes y Alvarez was born into poverty in Avila, Spain in 1542. His mother struggled after the death of her husband when John was only three and the death of her son Luis only two years later, most likely from malnutrition. She eventually found work and was able to feed John and his remaining brother, Francisco. She sent John to a school that provided a religious education as well as a bed, food, and clothing for orphans and children from poor families. From childhood, John knew he would enter religious life, and he attended a Jesuit school to complete his education. At the age of 21 he joined the Carmelite Order as John of St. Matthias. The Carmelites sent him to study theology and philosophy in Salamanca, where he committed the controversial act of translating the Song of Songs into Spanish, though Church rules prohibited the Bible from being translated from Latin.

> "How can you venture to live without fear, seeing that you must appear before God to give an account of your lightest words and thoughts?"
> – **St. John of the Cross**

John of St. Matthias was ordained in 1567 and found himself attracted to the simplicity of a cloistered life. When he met Teresa of Avila, a charismatic Carmelite nun, he admired her strict routine, simple life, and devotion to prayer, as well as her desire to reintroduce such practices to the Carmelite order. Her barefoot followers became known as the discalced Carmelites. On the day in 1568 that Teresa founded a new monastery, John renamed himself John of the Cross. Four years later, He accepted her invitation to come to Avila and become confessor and spiritual guide for Teresa and the other 130 nuns, a role he would fulfill for the next five years. During that period, John had a vision of Jesus on the cross looking down at him, which he captured in a drawing called *Christ from Above*, which still exists and inspired Salvador Dali's painting, *Christ of Saint John of the Cross*.

"Though the path is plain and smooth for men of good will, he who walks it will not travel far, and will do so only with difficulty, if he does not have good feet: that is, courage and a persevering spirit."
– **St. John of the Cross**

As a rift grew between the mainstream Carmelites and the Discalced Carmelites grew, John worked with Teresa to achieve her goal of restoring the original, stricter "Primitive Rule." She felt that the order became too liberal after the rule was relaxed by Pope Eugene IV in 1432. The conflict between the two Carmelite factions was escalated by the involvement of representatives from the Vatican and the political intrigues of the court of King Phillip II. In 1577, John disobeyed an order to leave Avila and return to his original house. His decision was based largely on the fact that his work to reform the Carmelite order had already been approved by the Papal Nuncio. He did not expect his decision to lead to being kidnapped from his residence by a group of Carmelites who took him under guard to the main house in Toledo where he was tried for disobedience and sentenced to imprisonment in the monastery.

"Behold how many there are who are called, and how few who are chosen! And behold, if you have no care for yourself, your perdition is more certain than your amendment, especially since the way that leads to eternal life is so narrow."
– **St. John of the Cross**

John's imprisonment in a tiny monastery cell was a spiritually and physically difficult time for him. He slept on the floor of a cell so small he could barely straighten his legs, and he lived on bread and water. He was subjected to weekly public lashings. He spent his time reading the prayer book he was allowed to keep and writing poetry on paper slipped to him by a guard. After his death, he would become known as an influential poet and was named the patron saint of Spanish poets. John finally escaped after nine months and joined Teresa's group of discalced Carmelites in Toledo. After recuperating in the hospital for more than a month, he went to Andalusia to serve as rector of a new college and to support the discalced Carmelites there. The rift ended the next year when Pope Gregory authorized the split and established the Discalced Carmelites as a separate order, which then numbered about 500 members (300 friars and 200 nuns) in 22 houses. John spent the last years of his life opening new houses throughout Spain.

> "Obedience is a penance of reason, and, on that account, a sacrifice more acceptable than all corporal penances and mortifications."
> – **St. John of the Cross**

One of the miracles attributed to St. John of the Cross during his lifetime occurred at the convent of the Incarnation, where he had been summoned to administer the Last Sacraments to a sister who was dying, but she passed before he arrived. He was chastised by one of the sisters, saying "Is this the way you take care of your children? This one has died without confession." John entered the church and begged God's help until he received word that the sister had been restored to life. On his way back to her bedside, John encountered the nun who had chastised him earlier, and he asked her, "My child, are you satisfied?" In the infirmary, he heard the now-living nun's confession and administered the Last Sacraments, and she soon passed away quietly.

> "Contemplation is nothing else than a secret, peaceful, and loving infusion of God, which if admitted, will set the soul on fire with the Spirit of love."
> – **St. John of the Cross**

In 1573, John of the Cross and Teresa of Avila were both in the parlor of the Incarnation on Trinity Sunday, on opposite sides of the grating, where they had been talking about the Most Blessed Trinity. When Sister Beatriz of Jesus entered with a message for Theresa, she saw her raised in the air, unaware of the presence of Sister Beatriz. Sister Beatriz called other sisters to witness Teresa's levitation, and they became aware of John of the Cross in a similar state on the other side of the grating. The explanation they arrived at was that the two had fallen into ecstasy simultaneously over their contemplation of the Most Blessed Trinity.

> "Whenever anything disagreeable or displeasing happens to you, remember Christ crucified and be silent."
> – **St. John of the Cross**

St. John of the Cross contracted an infection in an isolated Andalusian monastery and traveled to the monastery at Ubeda for medical care. Based on a description of his symptoms, it is likely that he was suffering from erysipelas, a staph infection similar to cellulitis that causes high fevers, tremors, chills, fatigue, vomiting, and headaches. Without antibiotics, which certainly weren't available in 1591, the prognosis was grim: sepsis and death, which was John's fate. Initially buried at Ubeda, his body was secretly moved to the monastery in Segovia, but the people of Ubeda petitioned Pope Clement VIII for its return. In a compromise, different parts of his body were assigned to each monastery as relics. John of the Cross was canonized in 1726 by Pope Benedict XIII and is the patron saint of contemplatives, mystics, and Spanish poets. Pope Pius XI declared St. John of the Cross a Doctor of the Church in 1926.

> "If you would rise, shun luxury, for luxury lowers and degrades."
> **– St. John Chrysostom**

John was not born with the name Chrysostom, which translates from the Greek as "golden-mouthed." In fact, the name does not appear in the historical record until 553, more than half a century after his death. It was used in recognition of the oratorical skills of the man who has been called the greatest Christian preacher ever. His reputation as an orator stemmed in part from his considerable natural talent for speaking, but is also reflects his intelligence, vast biblical knowledge, and deep conviction in his message, which he believed came to him from God. His homilies, delivered in an apparently spontaneous and entertaining manner, were often interrupted by applause from the congregation.

> "A comprehended god is no god."
> – **St. John Chrysostom**

John's mother was widowed shortly after his birth in 344 in Antioch, and she raised John and his older sister on her own. His early education in the best schools in Antioch befitted the son of a high-ranking officer in the Syrian army, with an emphasis on classical rather than ecclesiastical learning. The period in which John grew up was a troubled and chaotic one, rife with religious conflict among Pagans, Manichaeans, Arians, Gnostics, Apollinarians, Jews, and Christians. The Catholic Church itself was split between eastern and western bishops. Antioch, the second city of the Eastern part of the Roman Empire, was the backdrop for much turmoil during John's lifetime.

"If we knew that a place was unhealthy and subject to pestilence, would we not withdraw our children from it, without being stopped by the riches that they might heap up in it, or by the fact that their health had not as yet suffered? ... Among seculars shipwrecks are more frequent and sudden, because the difficulties of navigation are greater; but with anchorites storms are less violent, the calm is almost undisturbed. This is why we seek to draw as many as we can to the religious life."
– **St. John Chrysostom**

John's turn from classical and secular learning toward religious studies was inspired in large part by meeting the bishop Meletius when John was in his mid-twenties. He studied Scripture and the sermons of Meletius and within three years was ordained lector, or reader. But John sought spiritual perfection and entered an ascetic community where his time was spent in prayer, scriptural studies, manual labor, and writing on subjects related to asceticism and monasticism. Four years later, seeking an even more rigorous spiritual life, he became a hermit living in a cave near Antioch, with the apparent intention of remaining there indefinitely. However declining health due to extreme fasting and sleep deprivation forced his return to Antioch.

> "Necessity urges us to pray for ourselves. Fraternal Charity obliges us to pray for others. God finds the prayer motivated by charity to be more meritorious than the prayer motivated by necessity."
> – **St. John Chrysostom**

In early 381 or thereabouts, the bishop Meletius made John of Chrysostom deacon before leaving for Constantinople where he would die the same year. John developed a good relationship with Meletius' successor, Flavian, who ordained him as priest in 386. Shortly after he became a priest, there was civil unrest in Antioch over new taxes imposed by Emperor Theodosius, and when a mob tore down statues of the emperor, there was widespread fear of retaliation against the people of Antioch. Father John delivered a series of sermons meant to calm the public's fears and helped Bishop Flavian secure a pardon from the emperor. For the next dozen years, it fell upon John to do most of the religious instruction and education in Antioch. His many writings during this period helped secure his reputation as a renowned theological writer.

> "There is nothing colder than a Christian who is not concerned about the salvation of others ... Do not say, I cannot help others: for, if you are truly a Christian it is impossible not to."
> **– St. John Chrysostom**

Father John was probably on track to succeed Flavian as bishop of Antioch, but the bishop of Constantinople died first, leaving a void that Emperor Areadius need to fill without delay or controversy. Without the knowledge of the multiple competitors for the position, Emperor Areadius had John brought to Constantinople, announced that John would be the new bishop. The Patriarch of Alexandria, who had been supporting another candidate, ordained John Chrysostom as Bishop of Constantinople in 398. It was a sudden, unexpected change for John, but he wasted no time in trying to bring about reconciliation between eastern and western Catholics and reforming ecclesiastical life in Constantinople. He began by reducing expenses and increasing discipline, effectively "cleaning house" from top to bottom, first among the clergy and then among the people, regardless of class. Some people took offense at being rebuked for their excesses, but they flocked to hear his sermons. Learning that their new bishop used the savings from economizing in his own household to build a hospital was visible proof of his commitment to the poor and suffering.

> "Faithfulness in little things is a big thing."
> – **St. John Chrysostom**

Wealthy and noble citizens of Constantinople chafed at John's remonstrance over their moral failings and abuse of power. He had little patience with political intrigue or injustice, and his relationship with the Imperial Court became strained beginning around the year 401. The Empress and her courtiers found some allies among the ecclesiastical ranks, and when John left Constantinople for a few months to take care of an important Church matter, tensions between the Court and the See escalated, and plots abounded. Theophilis, Patriarch of Alexandria, conspired with some clerics who opposed Chrysostom and compiled a list of ludicrous charges against him. After considerable political machinations and maneuvering, John Chrysostom was deposed and exiled, not once but twice! His exile only increased the chaos. His followers were prosecuted for the conflagration that destroyed the cathedral, the senate building, and other landmarks in Constantinople. Those who refused to align themselves with the new archbishop faced the confiscation of their property and exile. Western Catholics sided with Chrysostom, and relations between east and west were worse than ever. Through it all, John Chrysostom held onto the hope of eventual vindication.

"As the body without the soul cannot love, so the soul without prayer is dead and emits an offensive odor."
— **St. John Chrysostom**

In exile, John Chrysostom was forced on several occasions to move farther away from Constantinople, and with each move, his living conditions became harsher. Finally, in the summer of 407, his removal to Pithyus, at the outermost edge of the empire, was ordered. The soldiers guarding him made the journey a literal death march, exposing John to the harshest of conditions and walking long distances with little sustenance. His health, already precarious, deteriorated quickly, but when he asked for a rest stop in Comana, he was forced to keep walking. The party hadn't gone far when John collapsed and was brought back to Comana, where he died within hours. Recognized as a Doctor of the Church, St. John Chrysostom is the patron saint of Constantinople, education, epileptics, lecturers, orators, and teachers.

"I ask you to consider that our Lord Jesus Christ is your true head and that you are a member of his body. He belongs to you as the head belongs to the body. All that is his is yours: breath, heart, body, soul and all his faculties. All of these you must use as if they belonged to you, so that in serving him you may give him praise, love and glory."
– **St. John Eudes**

At 32, John Eudes, a member of the community of Oratorians, began his work as a parish missionary in 1633. In 1643, he left the Oratorians and founded the Congregation of Jesus and Mary, known as the Eudists, because the Oratorians did not support his goal of founding seminaries to improve the instruction and spiritual formation of the clergy. The Eudists had some limited success in establishing seminaries but faced much opposition. In his parish mission work, John saw firsthand the plight of prostitutes who wanted to reform. Touched by their earnest desire to change their lives, he founded, with Madeleine Lamy, an advocate for fallen women, a religious community called the Sisters of Our Lady of Charity of the Refuge. In 1666 Alexander III approved the community as an institute for the care of penitent prostitutes. St. John Eudes is best known for his work with Sister Mary Margaret Alacoque to initiate devotion to the Sacred Heart of Jesus and the Holy Heart of Mary. He died in 1680 and was canonized in 1925 by Pope Pius XI.

> "If we look forward to receiving God's mercy, we can never fail to do good so long as we have the strength. For if we share with the poor, out of love for God, whatever he has given to us, we shall receive according to his promise a hundredfold in eternal happiness. What a fine profit, what a blessed reward!
> With outstretched arms he begs us to turn toward him, to weep for our sins, and to become the servants of love, first for ourselves, then for our neighbors. Just as water extinguishes a fire, so love wipes away sin."
> **– St. John of God**

John of God was born in 1495 and ran away at the age of 8 to travel with an itinerant priest. It was the first of the many impulsive moves that would shape the course of his life. His impulsive decisions led John to the brink of death on more than one occasion. After one particularly close call, he made a spur-of-the-moment vow to change his life, and though his impulses continued to rule his life, his rash actions from that point on were always aimed at helping others, though he often seemed eccentric if not irrational to observers. John's dramatic response to hearing a sermon on repentance caused him to behave so eccentrically that friends took him to the Royal Hospital where he was confined with the lunatics. The abusive treatment he experienced there, standard for the time, convinced him that God wanted him to found a hospital for the poor. John nursed and fed the sick and poor on the streets and in abandoned buildings until he was able to move his makeshift hospital into an old Carmelite monastery. He died on his 55th birthday of pneumonia contracted by jumping into a raging river to save a drowning boy. He is regarded as the founder of the Brothers Hospitallers.

> "Opting for peace does not mean a passive acquiescence to evil or compromise of principle. It demands an active struggle against hatred, oppression and disunity, but not by using methods of violence. Building peace requires creative and courageous action."
> – **Pope St. John Paul II**

Pope John Paul II, elected in 1978, became the first non-Italian pope in 455 years and the first ever from a Slavic country. Canonized only nine years after his death in 2005, he was a contemporary of many people alive today. His papacy and his travels received extensive media coverage, making him familiar to Catholics and non-Catholics alike. Born Karol J. Wojtyla in Wadowice, Poland in 1920, he'd lost both parents and his only sibling by the time he reached adulthood. His college education was interrupted by the Nazi occupation, and Karol labored in a quarry and a chemical factory while preparing for the priesthood by studying at an "underground" seminary run by Cardinal Sapieha, the archbishop of Cracow. Once the war ended, he was able to complete his undergraduate education and was ordained on November 1, 1946 before going to Rome to earn his Doctorate of Theology. He earned a second doctorate in philosophy in 1953 and taught philosophy at the University of Lublin. Five years later, Communist authorities approved his appointment as auxiliary bishop of Krakow, believing Karol to be an apolitical intellectual. Little did they know that he espoused nonviolent political activism and would support the rise of the Solidarity Movement in the 1980s and contribute to the dissolution of the Soviet Union in 1999.

> "Only in Christ can men and women find answers to the ultimate questions that trouble them. Only in Christ can they fully understand their dignity as persons created and loved by God."
> **– Pope St. John Paul II**

Pope John Paul II drew enormous crowds wherever he went. Even as Parkinson's Disease sapped his strength, he continued to travel and conducted Mass for crowds numbering in the millions – an estimated four million in Manila in 1995. The crowds loved him, and he loved them as well. He had a special fondness for young people and for spending time in their company. As a priest, he would take local youth on camping trips, singing and praying with them around a campfire. Even as a bishop and cardinal, he spent time with young people whenever he could and was sometimes referred to as an eternal teenager. He said, "I believe in youth with all my heart and with all the strength of my conviction." Young people responded to his authenticity and obvious love for humanity and God, and St. John Paul II drew comfort and strength from them.

Opting for peace does not mean a passive acquiescence to evil or compromise of principle. It demands an active struggle against hatred, oppression and disunity, but not by using methods of violence. Building peace requires creative and courageous action.
– Pope St. John Paul II

The two miracles required for the canonization of Pope John Paul II were both healing miracles. The first was the healing of a French nun who had prayed for his intercession in relieving her suffering from Parkinson's Disease, the same disease that afflicted John Paul II. Her healing in 2005 was determined to have no medical explanation. The second miracle was the 2011 healing of a Costa Rican woman suffering partial paralysis and severe pain from an inoperable aneurysm that her doctor said could kill her at any moment. She had a vision of John Paul II while she was holding a magazine that bore his picture on the cover. In the vision, she heard him speak to her, and his hands appeared to reach out toward her from the magazine cover. After this vision, her neurosurgeon could find no evidence of the aneurysm. John Paul II was canonized during the same ceremony as Pope John XXIII in 2014.

"Freedom exists for the sake of love."
 – Pope St. John Paul II

These words of St. Pope John Paul II remind us that God's great gift to us, free will, enables us to give Him the gift of loving Him and doing good in the world by choice, not by command. He doesn't force us to obey His laws or do His will on Earth. We do so by choice, not under duress or out of fear other than the fear of not spending eternity with Him. Allowing us to choose between good and evil is proof of God's immense love for us, and when we choose good, we are acting out of our love for Him. John Paul II's sentiment is reminiscent of a popular but anonymous quote, often repeated and featured on posters and wall hangings and greeting cards: "If you love something, set it free. If it comes back, it is yours. If it doesn't, it never was." God sets us free and those who love Him find their way back to Him.

> "When you approach the tabernacle remember that he has been waiting for you for twenty centuries."
> **– St. Josemaria Escriva**

St. Josemaria Escriva de Blaguer is best known for founding Opus Dei (Work of God) in 1928, three years after his ordination. Its genesis was divinely inspired and revealed to Father Escriva during a retreat. The movement was the outward expression of his belief that ordinary lay people gain in holiness by carrying out their daily tasks with a Christian spirit and obedience to God's will. Father Escriva continued ministering to the sick and the poor during Spain's Civil War, but had to be clandestine about his activities and not remain in one place for too long. After the war, he completed his doctorate in law in Madrid and later earned a doctorate in theology in Rome. Opus Dei continued to thrive and grow, becoming in 1983 the first, and so far the only, personal prelature—a canonical structure comprising a prelate, clergy, and laity with a specific pastoral mission.

"Don't you long to shout to those youths who are bustling around you: 'Fools! Leave those worldly things that shackle the heart – and very often degrade it – leave all that and come with us in search of Love!'"
– **St. Josemaria Escriva**

In 1943, Father Escriva established the Priestly Society of the Holy Cross to enable some of the lay members of Opus Dei to become ordained as priests. In addition to serving the spiritual needs of the Opus Dei community, the Priestly Society works with local bishops to further the spiritual development of diocesan priests and seminarians. At the same time, diocesan priests could join the Priestly Society while still serving in their own dioceses. In 1948, married people became able to gain full membership in Opus Dei, and beginning in 1950, non-Catholics and even non-Christians could become Opus Dei cooperators, helping further its mission without being members.

"We have approached the fire of the love of God. Let us allow that fire to burn our lives. Let us feed the desire to spread that divine fire throughout the world, making it known to all the people around us. They too can experience the peace of Christ and find happiness there. A Christian who lives united to Christ's heart can have no goals but these: peace in society, peace in the Church, peace in his soul, the peace of God which will reach its climax when his kingdom comes."
– **St. Josemaria Escriva**

From 1970 until his death in 1975, Josemaria, now Monsignor Escriva, traveled throughout Europe and South America spreading the message of Opus Dei about the sanctification of work and family life. By the time of his death, Opus Dei could be found in thirty nations on every continent but Antarctica. As of 2016, there were 94,776 members of the Opus Dei Prelature in more than 90 countries—92,667 lay members and 2,109 priests, not including the diocesan priests belonging to Opus Dei's Priestly Society of the Holy Cross. Monsignor Escriva was canonized in October 2002 by Pope John Paul II, who commended him for "inviting Christians to be united to God through their daily work."

> "Heaven is filled with converted sinners of all kinds, and there is room for more."
> – **St. Joseph Cafasso**

Father Joseph Cafasso (1811-1860) was much sought after as a confessor and spiritual advisor and fulfilled that role for his lifelong friend, St. John Bosco. It was a role Father Joseph also took on in working with prisoners. He worked to improve the living conditions of the incarcerated, but he also aimed to save their souls. The spiritual guidance and comfort he provided to those awaiting execution for their crimes earned him the nickname, "The Priest of the Gallows." He encouraged them to confess, even demanded that they do so, before the death sentence was carried out, so that they might know God's mercy. On one occasion, he heard confession from 60 converted prisoners who were condemned, most of whom were hanged immediately after receiving absolution, and referred to thereafter by Father Cafasso as "hanged saints." Canonized in 1947, St. Joseph Cafasso is the patron of prisoners, Italian prisoners, condemned prisoners, and prison chaplains.

> "Clearly, what God wants above all is our will which we received as a free gift from God in creation and possess as though our own. When a man trains himself to acts of virtue, it is with the help of grace from God from whom all good things come that he does this. The will is what man has as his unique possession."
> **– St. Joseph of Cupertino**

Joseph was born in Cupertino, Italy in 1603. Thought by all who knew him to be clumsy and slow-witted, and with no education other than a failed apprenticeship to a shoemaker, Joseph entered a Capuchin monastery as a lay brother at the age of 17 and was dismissed eight months later. His parents were dismayed at his return home, as he had never given them anything but trouble and embarrassment. His mother harangued her brother, a Franciscan of some local standing, until he agreed to admit his nephew to the local monastery as a servant. In time, the Franciscan brothers came to see Joseph's kind heart, simple but unwavering faith, and unflagging spirit and he was eventually allowed to study for the priesthood. He was ordained as a priest when he was 25. He is best known as a mystic who was reportedly observed more than 70 times levitating in rapture during Mass or while praying. He performed so many miracles and drew so many people looking for a miracle that he was kept out of public sight to the extent possible. He died in 1663 and was canonized by Pope Clement XIII in 1767. Because of his many experiences with levitation, St. Joseph of Cupertino is the patron saint of pilots and airplane passengers, as well as of the learning disabled.

> "All my life I have wanted to be a missionary. I have wanted to carry the gospel message to those who have never heard of God and the kingdom he has prepared for them."
> – **St. Junipero Serra**

Brother Junipero Serra, a Franciscan, spent the first 34 years of his life as a student and then as a professor in his native Spain. At 35 he decided to pursue his goal of converting indigenous people in the New World. For the next 18 years he did just that in Central America and the Baja Peninsula. When King Charles III of Spain learned of a Russian expedition heading south from present-day Alaska to claim land along the Pacific coast, he ordered his own expedition to beat them to it. Brother Junipero accompanied the conquistador, José de Galvez, northward along the coast, establishing missions along the way, beginning with San Diego in 1769, followed by Monterey/Carmel, San Antonio, San Gabriel, San Luís Obispo, San Francisco, San Juan Capistrano, Santa Clara, and San Buenaventura. The missions provided a sort of communal living for his converts. He sought and won legal protection from the Spanish crown for the Indians and the missions. During his years in the New World, Brother Junipero baptized over 6,000 people and confirmed 5,000, earning their love and respect in the process. He was canonized in 2015 by Pope Francis.

> "If all could know the happiness of the religious state, men would rush madly into it."
> **– St. Lawrence Justinian**

There were several saints among Lawrence's ancestors, and his mother, a devout Catholic, imparted her faith to him when he was a child. He always planned on a religious life, and he entered the monastery of the Canons Regular of St. Augustine, near Venice, when he was nineteen. The monks admired him for his fervent prayers and mortifications, and despite his youth, he was made prior shortly after his ordination and became general of the congregation soon after that. He rooted out corruption and brought about such profound reforms that he was regarded as the order's second founder. In 1433 at the age of 52, he was made Bishop of Castello. During his time in that position, he implemented many reforms, founded 15 new monasteries, and added many parishes. In 1451 Lawrence Justinian became the first Patriarch of Venice, a position he held until his death in 1456 at age 74. He was canonized in 1690 by Pope Alexander VIII.

"True and certain is that Hope which is accompanied by good works. But if it goes alone, it ought to be called presumption."
– **St. Lawrence Justinian**

Lawrence was known for his piety, Christian charity, and generosity toward the poor, while living very simply himself. When it became clear that he was gravely ill, his servants made up a more comfortable bed for him, but he insisted on being laid on his usual one, which he believed to be more like Christ's hard deathbed – the Cross. Lawrence was patient and kind, but he eschewed sentimentalism and had been regarded since childhood as serious and focused. Those qualities were exactly what people of his time looked for in a leader, though Lawrence did not aspire to be one. He reigned as Patriarch of Venice during the time that Muslim forces conquered Constantinople, a close trading partner of Venice for centuries, and he was a calming influence for a city of people panicking about their future.

"I thank God that I have not a penny in the world to dispose of."
– **St. Lawrence O'Toole** (on his deathbed when asked if he had a will.)

St. Lawrence O'Toole (c. 1125 – 1180) was the son of the chief of the Murray clan in Kildare, Ireland, and became the first Irish-born archbishop of Dublin in 1161. It was a time of great change for the Catholic Church in Ireland with the end of Scandinavian influence in Dublin and subsequent invasion of Ireland by the English. Lawrence aimed to strengthen the relationship between the Irish Church and Rome. Lawrence proved to be an adept negotiator and was held in high esteem by all the parties vying for influence in Ireland. The Irish, Vikings, and Normans all viewed him as a man of honor and integrity. It was on a mission to King Henry II of England that Lawrence died in Normandy, France. He was canonized in 1225. In addition to the many reforms he brought about, Lawrence was known for his great humility, austerity, and strict observance of rules. He was known to wear a hair shirt beneath his episcopal garb and spent 40 days of every year secluded in the cave in Glendalough where St. Kevin had lived as a hermit in the 6th century.

> "Virtue is nothing without the trial of temptation, for there is no conflict without an enemy, no victory without strife."
> – **Pope St. Leo the Great**

During Leo's reign as pope, Attila and his Huns invaded Italy, leaving devastation in their wake as they made their way toward Rome. Attila reportedly demanded that the emperor's sister, Honoria, be sent to him with a dowry. Emperor Valentinian III refused to hand his sister over to the barbarians and sent Leo and two other envoys to negotiate with Attila outside of the city. Attila did withdraw after that meeting, but his reasons for doing so are the subject of much speculation. Just a few years later, Leo was unable to prevent the city being sacked by the King Genseric's Vandals, but his intercession with Generic prevented Rome from being burned, which saved the lives of the many Romans who had sought sanctuary inside the Basilicas of St. Peter, St. Paul, and St. John.

"By Baptism we are made flesh of the Crucified"
– **Pope St. Leo the Great**

The exact date of Leo's birth is unknown, but it was probably around the year 400. He was a Roman aristocrat born in the Tuscany region of Italy. His first appearances in the historical record date to his time as a deacon. It is clear from the fact that he was sent to negotiate several disputes on behalf of the Imperial Court that he had the emperor's confidence. When Pope Sixtus III died, Leo was in Gaul trying to settle a dispute between a military commander and the chief magistrate. The people unanimously elected Leo pope in his absence.

"The faith of those who live their faith is a serene faith. What you long for will be given you; what you love will be yours forever. Since it is by giving alms that everything is pure for you, you will also receive that blessing which is promised next by the Lord: The Godhead that no man has been able to see. In the inexpressible joy of this eternal vision, human nature will possess what eye has not seen or ear heard, what man's heart has never conceived."
– **Pope St. Leo the Great**

Leo was emphatic that the Church was built on Peter and that the pope acted on behalf of Peter. Perhaps the most significant aspect of his pontificate was his assertion of the universal jurisdiction of the Roman bishop, or the doctrine of Petrine supremacy. Before his death, Pope Leo expressed his wish to be buried as close as possible to St. Peter's tomb. Upon Leo's death in 461, he was entombed in the portico of St. Peter's basilica. Over two hundred years later, his remains were moved inside the basilica. Pope Benedict VIV named Leo a Doctor of the Church in 1754.

> "If you practice the holy exercise of Spiritual Communion a good many times each day, within a month you will see yourself completely changed."
> – **St. Leonard of Port Maurice**

Father Leonard Casanova had a gift for preaching. He spoke plainly and frequently used the stations of the cross to illustrate his talks. During his many years of preaching, he built stations of the cross all over Italy, 571 sets to be exact, including one in the Coliseum where so many early Christians were martyred. He was also sought after as a spiritual director, and his letters to his advisees reflect a commonsense Christianity that even ordinary people found very accessible. Born Paul Jerome Casanova in Porto Maurizio on the northwestern coast of Italy in 1676, he took the name Brother Leonard when he joined the Franciscans of the Strict Observance in 1697. He spent over 40 years preaching retreats and parish missions all over Italy, making converts wherever he went. He often held his parish mission meetings outdoors because the crowds he attracted were too large to fit into the local churches. When he was sent by Pope Benedict XIV on diplomatic missions, officials were surprised to find that the papal representative was a humble, barefoot friar. He died in Rome at age 74 in 1751 and was canonized in 1867. St. Leonard of Port Maurice is the patron of parish priests.

"Pray with great confidence, with confidence based upon the goodness and infinite generosity of God and upon the promises of Jesus Christ. God is a spring of living water which flows unceasingly into the hearts of those who pray."
– **St. Louis de Montfort**

The life of Louis Marie Grignon, born in Montfort, France in 1673, was devoted to Mary, the Blessed Mother. He was ordained a diocesan priest in 1700 and spent years ministering to the poor and preaching parish missions after Pope Clement XI gave him the title of Apostolic Missionary. His message was simple—accepting God's will for one's life as the Virgin Mary did. He founded two congregations, the Missionaries of the Company of Mary for priests and other male religious practitioners and the Daughters of Wisdom, dedicated to providing care for the ill. He also established several free schools for poor children. While his missions brought thousands back to the faith, they also garnered complaints from Church authorities because Louis recommended daily Holy Communion, which was not the custom. Louis died in 1716 after a brief illness at the age of 43, having accomplished much in his brief 16 years as a priest. Stories of miracles occurring among those who prayed at his tomb began to circulate shortly after his burial in the parish church in Saint-Laurent-sur-Sevre. He was canonized in 1947.

> "The Rosary is a priceless treasure inspired by God."
> **– St. Louis De Monfort**

St. John Paul II credited St. Louis de Montfort for his choice of "Totus Tuus," or "totally thine," as his apostolic motto. He explained in *Crossing the Threshold of Hope* that his personal consecration to Mary was based on the spiritual approach of St. Louis de Montfort: "Thanks to St. Louis de Montfort, I came to understand that true devotion to the Mother of God is actually Christocentric; indeed, it is very profoundly rooted in the mystery of the Blessed Trinity and the mysteries of the Incarnation and Redemption." As a seminarian, the pontiff had read and reread the writings of de Montfort. John Paul II borrowed the phrase "totus tuus" from a prayer he found in de Montfort's book, *True Devotion to Mary*. The prayer begins (in Latin) with these words, "Totus tuus ergo sum, et omnia mea tua sunt," which translate as "I belong entirely to you, and all that I have is yours." The prayer concludes with "I take you for my all. O Mary, give me your heart."

"Angel of God and well-beloved brother, I trust myself to your beneficence and implore you humbly to intercede for me with my Spouse, so that He may forgive me my sins, strengthen me in well-doing, help me by His grace to correct my faults, and lead me to Paradise, there to taste the fruition of His presence and to possess eternal life. Amen."
– **St. Lydwina of Schiedam**

At the age of 15, Lydwina, born into a large working-class family in Schiedam, Holland, fell while ice skating and broke her rib. It marked the beginning of a steady physical decline that culminated in her death at the age of 54. Scientists today believe she may have suffered from multiple sclerosis, which would make her case the first recorded instance of the disease. Throughout her life, Lydwina suffered headaches, vomiting, muscle spasms, extreme thirst, neuritis, blindness, paralysis, and more, with brief periods of remission. Bedridden much of the time, she became known as a mystic who experienced supernatural visions and the stigmata. She bore her suffering as the will of God and offered up her pain as atonement for the sins of all humanity. She was confirmed a saint in 1890 by Pope Leo XIII and is the patron of the chronically ill, skaters, and her hometown of Schiedam.

"As iron is fashioned by fire and on the anvil, so in the fire of suffering and under the weight of trials our souls receive that form which our Lord desires them to have."
– **St. Madeline-Sophie Barat**

Born in the French village of Joigny in 1779, Madeline-Sophie Barat received her early education from her older brother, a priest. She and three other young women were accepted into religious life by a priest her brother recommended her to, who envisioned a female counterpart of the Society of Jesus, or Jesuits. They formed the Society of the Sacred Heart of Jesus in 1800 with two goals: revealing God's love to the world and educating children to be a source of transformation in the world. They founded a convent and school in 1801, and the following year, Madeline was named Superior though she was only 23. She held that position for 63 years. During that time the Society grew and established communities throughout France—more than 100 houses and schools in 12 countries. By the time of her death in 1865, there were 3,359 women in the Society of the Sacred Heart of Jesus, and today there are more than 2,500 members in provinces in 41 countries. St. Madeline-Sophie Barat was canonized in 1925.

"We should always look to God as in ourselves, no matter in what manner we meditate upon Him, so as to accustom ourselves to dwell in His divine presence. For when we behold Him within our souls, all our powers and faculties, and even our senses, are recollected within us. If we look at God apart from ourselves, we are easily distracted by exterior objects."
– **St. Margaret Mary Alacoque**

Margaret Alacoque was born in 1647 in L'Hautecour, France, the daughter of a notary who would die of pneumonia when she was only eight years old. Her parents were devout Catholics who imparted their values to their daughter, who soon showed a preference for prayer and silence over childhood games. After her father's death, Margaret was sent to the school operated by the Poor Clares at Charolles, where she secretly practiced corporal mortifications. Her piety impressed the nuns and she was allowed to make her First Communion at the age of nine, several years ahead of what was the custom at the time. A bout of rheumatic fever left her bedridden from the age of ten until she was fifteen. During her illness she developed a profound devotion to the Blessed Sacrament.

> "Believe me, do not be cast down or grieved at the small vexations by which it pleases our Lord to try your love and patience; but endeavor rather to conform your will to His, letting Him do with you according to His desire, which is, that you should remain peaceful and resigned in the midst of your difficulties."
> **– St. Margaret Mary Alacoque**

The Alacoque family's circumstances were drastically altered by the death of Claude, Margaret's father. He had not managed his money well and left his wife and children with little to live on. When Margaret was returned to recuperate from complications of rheumatic fever, it was to a household that had been taken over by relatives of her father. Margaret and her mother, Philiberte, were treated as little more than servants. Once Margaret recovered, her relatives controlled when she could leave the house and where she could go, and she often cried over her inability to go to church very often. It was a difficult time for Margaret, but everything improved when her eldest brother reached the age of majority and control of the property reverted to him.

> "In order to make good use of time, we must love ardently and constantly; we must surrender ourselves entirely to love, leaving it to act for us. Be satisfied to adhere to it in everything but always with profound humility."
> – **St. Margaret Mary Alacoque**

For a brief period in her teens, encouraged by her brothers, Margaret began to go out into the world and participate in activities commonly enjoyed by young ladies of her age and station. Throughout her life she agonized over having worn jewelry and a carnival mask—acts she deemed frivolous and sinful. When she returned from a ball one evening, Christ appeared to her in a vision, bleeding from his scourging and chastising her for being unfaithful to him. Shortly thereafter, Margaret rebuffed her mother's attempts to arrange a marriage for her and entered the Visitation convent at Paray-le-Monial, taking the name Margaret Mary.

"I am very glad that our divine Master has shown you that these trials add to the burden of your office; for He wishes them to be the cause of your having more frequent recourse to His Goodness, which will turn all these things to His glory and to your advantage, if you second His designs."
– **St. Margaret Mary Alacoque,** to a Superioress

Sister Margaret Mary chose to impose suffering upon herself in the form of corporal mortifications as she had when she was younger. One of her greatest desires was to suffer, as she had nothing to give the Lord other than her love. She offered her suffering to Him as proof of her love and her willingness to die to be united with Him. It was a practice she continued throughout her life. She also believed that by sharing the sufferings of souls in Purgatory, she would rescue them from the fires.

"You see plainly that I do not mean to advise you to perform great austerities, but rather generously to mortify your passions and inclinations, detaching your heart and emptying it of all that is earthly, and exercising charity towards your neighbor and liberality towards the poor."
– **St. Margaret Mary Alacoque**

Margaret Mary experienced her first vision of Christ on December 27, 1673. She described a feeling of being suffused by the Divine Presence and reported that Christ invited her to take the place occupied by St. John at the Last Supper, at His right hand. The Lord told her she would be the instrument through which he would reveal the love and graces of His heart to mankind. Margaret Mary would continue to receive the Lord's revelations over the next eighteen months.

"Our Lord Jesus Christ desires that we should, for sanctifying ourselves, glorify His all-loving Heart; for it was His Heart that suffered the most in His Sacred Humanity."
– **St. Margaret Mary Alacoque**

It was during her conversations with Christ that He gave Margaret Mary the mission of establishing the devotion to His Sacred Heart. Her efforts to carrying out His instructions to perform specific devotions, brought her much criticism, and her superior, Mother de Saumaise, commanded Margaret Mary to live the common life in accordance with the maxim of the Visitation order's founder, St. Jane Frances de Chantal, "not to be extraordinary except by being ordinary." Though her humility and charity toward her critics eventually won over Mother de Saumaise, others in the community continued in their opposition to Margaret Mary's ideas, and a group of theologians considering her delusional, advised her to adopt a healthier diet.

"I can say nothing more, except that the effacement of yourself will raise you to union with your Sovereign Good. By forgetting self, you will possess Him, and by yielding yourself up to Him, He will possess you."
– **St. Margaret Mary Alacoque**

One of the devotions Margaret Mary was instructed by Christ to implement was to lie prostrate from 11:00 pm to midnight on the eve of the first Friday of every month, to share in His loneliness and sorrow in Gethsemane, and to receive Holy Communion on that Friday. He also commanded her to establish the feast of the Sacred Heart. It was not until 1683 when a new superior was named and appointed Margaret Mary as her assistant that the opposition to her efforts to obey these instructions ceased. The convent first observed the feast of the Sacred Heart privately in 1686, after Margaret Mary had become Mistress of Novices. Two years later a chapel dedicated to the Sacred Heart was built on convent grounds.

"The Sacred Heart of Christ is an inexhaustible fountain and its sole desire is to pour itself out into the hearts of the humble so as to free them and prepare them to lead lives according to his good pleasure."
– St. Margaret Mary Alacoque

One of the instructions Margaret Mary was given by Christ was for Louis IV to consecrate the nation of France to His Sacred Heart. He did not, and neither did his successor, Louis XV. Louis XVI did consecrate France to the Sacred Heart before his imprisonment during the French Revolution, but it was too late to save himself and his queen from the guillotine or France from the violence and turmoil that would continue for another six years.

> "It seems to me that the happiness of a soul consists entirely in conforming to the most adorable Will of God; for in so doing the heart finds peace and the spirit joy and repose, since he 'who is joined to the Lord in one spirit' with Him." (1 Cor. 6:17).
> – **St. Margaret Mary Alacoque**

Much of what is known about the life of St. Margaret Mary Alacoque comes from her autobiography and from the letters she wrote to her superior, to other sisters, and to those who wrote to her inquiring about the Sacred Heart. St. Claude La Colombiere, her confessor at the time the Lord made His revelations about His Sacred Heart, recorded the details of each visitation as Margaret Mary described them to him. These accounts incorporate the words of the Lord, which Mary Margaret was able to recall and repeat in great detail after each vision, including the twelve promises of the Sacred Heart.

"Affliction or consolation, health or sickness, is all one to a heart that loves. Since we wish only to please God, it should be enough for us that His Will is accomplished."
– **St. Margaret Mary Alacoque**

Margaret Mary died in 1690, and Pope Clement XIII approved the devotion to the Sacred Heart 75 years later. She was canonized in 1920. St. Margaret Mary Alacoque, St. John Eudes, and St. Claude La Colombiere are known as the Saints of the Sacred Heart. St. Claude La Colombiere served for a time as the confessor for the Visitation convent at Paray-le-Monial and declared Margaret Mary's visions genuine when others were skeptical.

> "Trials are nothing else but the forge that purifies the soul of all its imperfections."
> – **St. Mary Magdalene de'Pazzi**

St. Mary Magdalene was born Catherine in 1566 in Florence, Italy, into the wealthy and noble de'Pazzi family. When Catherine was nine, the family chaplain, at the request of her mother, taught her a form of prayer that involved 30 minutes of meditation. When she was twelve, viewing a spectacular sunset with her mother, Catherine experienced the first of the many ecstasies that would continue throughout her life. Shortly after making her First Communion, she made a vow of lifelong virginity, and when she was ready to enter religious life, she looked specifically for a monastery where the nuns took Communion every day, which was not the norm at the time. She found what she was looking for in the Carmelite monastery of St. Mary's of the Angels. She entered the monastery at the age of 16, taking the name Mary Magdalene, and soon had the second of the mystical experiences that would eventually result in her being known as the "ecstatic saint." Her confessor, to ensure the authenticity of her revelations and provide a written record of them, instructed her to dictate them to the other sisters. During the next six years, the sisters filled five large volumes documenting Sister Mary Magdalene's mystical experiences.

> "Oh! Could you but see the beauty of a soul in the grace of God, you would be so much enamored of it that you would do nothing else but ask souls of God; and, on the contrary, could a soul in mortal sin be placed before your eyes, you would do nothing but weep, and you would hate sin more than the devil himself and always pray for the conversion of sinners."
> – **St. Mary Magdalene de'Pazzi**

Sister Mary Magdalene suffered greatly throughout her life. She regarded her frequent illnesses, emotional pain, self-doubt, spiritual torment, and self-inflicted corporal punishments as gifts from God intended to help her become more obedient, holy, and worthy of His love. Though she was initially refused early profession, she was allowed to profess from a stretcher at the altar when she became seriously ill. Her symptoms continued to worsen during the forty days of ecstasies that ensued and were only relieved when she requested the intercession of Blessed Mary Bagnesi. Her revelations during that forty-day period filled an entire volume of the record being maintained by the sisters of St. Mary's of the Angels. Her dictated account shows the personal relationship of Mary Magdalene's relationship with Christ. In one often quoted example, Jesus repeatedly offered her a choice between a crown of thorns and a crown of flowers. She always chose the crown of thorns, and Jesus kept pushing the crown of flowers toward her, as if teasing her. When he finally said, "I called you and you didn't care," she responded, "You didn't call loudly enough." During the five years of spiritual trial that followed, and long afterward, Mary Magdalene flagellated herself with a crown of thorns and was known to secure thorns and nails beneath her clothing to suffer as Christ had suffered.

> "A single instant passed under simple obedience is immeasurably more valuable in the sight of God than an entire day spent in the most sublime contemplation."
> – **St. Mary Magdalene de'Pazzi**

Sister Mary Magdalene was embarrassed by the attention she received as a result of her mystical experiences. She tried to hide her suffering and her penances from others even as she fulfilled her ever-increasing responsibilities within the monastery. She eventually concluded that although she would have preferred a "hidden life," God wanted something different from her. As mistress of novices, she shared her wisdom with the young women under her supervision, often quite bluntly. She saw no reason to sugarcoat the truth when she thought a sister's spiritual life was endangered. For example, when a novice asked permission to feign impatience so as not to be prideful of the respect her fellow novices accorded her, Mary Magdalene told her, "They don't respect you nearly as much as you like to think." She was equally honest, with herself and with others, about her own challenges and failings, acknowledging that the greatest penance for her was pretending to like something she didn't like, though the pretense provided the additional benefit of allowing her to do penance without anyone knowing she was doing it. It was one way in which she was able to enjoy the hidden life she craved.

"You will be consoled according to the greatness of your sorrow and affliction; the greater the suffering, the greater will be the reward."
– St. Mary Magdalene de'Pazzi

Sister Mary Magdalene spent her last three years as a bedridden invalid, suffering extreme physical pain until her death in 1607, at the age of 41. During her lifetime, there were several instances of bilocation, as she appeared to people far from the monastery she never left, and there were reports of healing miracles before and after her death. She was also said to have been able to discern the unspoken thoughts of others and to predict future events. The process of beatification began only three years after her death and was completed sixteen years later, in 1626. She was canonized in 1669 by Pope Clement IX. St. Mary Magdalene de'Pazzi is well-known in Italy, particularly in her native Florence and among Carmelites throughout the world. The lesson to be learned from her life is one of love and its role in uniting the soul to God.

"Good example is the most efficacious apostolate. You must be as lighted lanterns and shine like brilliant chandeliers among men. By your good example and your words, animate others to know and love God."
– **St. Mary Joseph Rossello**

Benedetta Rossello, born in 1811 in a small seaport in Liguria, Italy, spent seven years working for a wealthy couple before making the decision to enter a convent. Her lack of a dowry was an impediment to entering the convent, one her childless employers were reluctant to remove because they loved her and had hoped to make her their heir. She became a Franciscan tertiary at 16 and gained a reputation for instructing young girls in the Catholic faith. In 1837, the bishop of Savona enabled Mary Joseph (Benedetta's religious name) and three companions to found a community in Savona by purchasing a house and equipping it as a school. Mary Joseph, remembering her own difficulties due to the lack of a dowry, did not require one for young women entering the Institute of the Daughters of Our Lady of Mercy, which was devoted to the education of poor young women, caring for the sick, and other charitable works. Mother Mary Joseph served as superior of the community for forty years, establishing 68 foundations before her death in 1888.

> "The soul is regenerated in the sacred waters of baptism and thus becomes God's child."
> – **St. Maximilian Kolbe**

Raymund Kolbe's childhood was unremarkable except for one significant event that foreshadowed his ultimate martyrdom at the hands of the Nazis. As a boy of 12, he had a dream in which Our Lady offered him the choice of two crowns: one white and one red. She asked which he was willing to accept, the white one meaning a life of purity or the red one that meant he would become a martyr. His answer was that he would accept both, and his life reflected that choice. Torn between military and religious life, he became a spiritual warrior. He maintained a lifelong devotion to the Blessed Virgin, actively promoting the Immaculate Virgin Mary and organizing the Militia Immaculata, or Army of the Immaculate One, working for the conversion of Freemasons and other enemies of the church through the intercession of Mary. Even when he knew his death was imminent, he led his fellow prisoners in Auschwitz in prayers to Our Lady. His devotion to Mary earned him the title the Apostle of Consecration to Mary.

"In all things let us not forget to repeat with the Lord Jesus: 'Not my will but Thine be done'... Let us not forget that Jesus not only suffered, but also rose in glory; so, too, we go to the glory of the Resurrection by way of suffering and the Cross."
– **St. Maximilian Kolbe**

As a Polish Conventual Franciscan friar, Raymund Kolbe, who took the religious name Maximilian, accomplished much in the years before his imprisonment by the Nazis. He earned doctorates in both philosophy and theology, funded a monthly magazine called "Knight of the Immaculate," ran a religious publishing operation and founded a new Conventual Franciscan monastery in Niepokalanow, Poland, as well as one in Nagasaki, Japan and one in India. Poor health forced him to return to Poland, and he would be one of the few brothers to remain in the monastery after the German invasion. Maximilian did whatever he could to relieve suffering during the war, including establishing an infirmary, providing shelter for 2,000 Jews, and publishing anti-Nazi materials. When the Nazis shut down the monastery in 1941, he was arrested, imprisoned for three months in Pawiak, and then transferred to Auschwitz, where the final chapter of his life would unfold.

"The most deadly poison of our times is indifference. And this happens, although the praise of God should know no limits. Let us strive, therefore, to praise Him to the greatest extent of our powers."
– **St. Maximilian Kolbe**

After only a few weeks Maximilian, prisoner #16670, witnessed ten men being taken from his barracks, chosen to die by starvation as punishment for another prisoner's escape and to serve as an example to all. Maximilian offered to take the place of one of the men who had a family, knowing that he would face weeks of suffering before he died. He ministered to the other starving prisoners until, after three weeks of agony, he and the three others still living were executed by injections of carbolic acid. Franciszek Gajowniczek, the man whose place Maximilian had taken, survived five years in Auschwitz and was present in St. Peter's Square in 1982, when the man who had saved his life was declared St. Maximilian Kolbe by Pope John Paul II.

> "Some passions pertain to the soul's incensive power, and others to its desiring aspect. Both kinds are aroused through the senses. They are aroused when the soul lacks love and self-control."
> – **St. Maximos the Confessor**

Maximos, born around 580 (probably near Constantinople), gave up his political life as an aide to the Byzantine Emperor Heraclius to enter a monastery. An avid student of philosophy, he was drawn into a theological controversy that pitted the view that Christ has two natures (human and divine) but only one will, a divine one (monothelitism) against the view that Christ has two natures and two wills, both human and divine (dyothelitism). Maximos supported the latter position, and for that he was persecuted. As punishment, he suffered mutilation of his tongue and right hand and was exiled.

> "When you are insulted by someone or humiliated, guard against angry thoughts, lest they arouse a feeling of irritation, and so cut you off from love and place you in the realm of hatred."
> – **St. Maximos the Confessor**

There are few confirmed facts about the life of Maximos prior to his involvement in the political and theological controversy over whether Christ's two natures, human and divine, meant that He had both human and divine wills. It is likely that he spent his youth near Constantinople because of his exceptional education. It is also likely that he was born into an aristocratic family because by the age of 30 he had attained a position of trust as an aide to the Byzantine Emperor. That would probably not have been the case if he had been low-born. Among the few autobiographical details included in his writings are the facts that he never studied rhetoric and took his monastic vows at the monastery of Phillippicus, where he later served as abbot. The Persian conquest forced Maximus to flee to a monastery near Carthage, where he continued his theological studies and writing. He became a popular figure there and was called upon unofficially to provide political and spiritual advice to leaders in North Africa.

"'Shun evil and do good' (Ps. 34:14), that is to say, fight the enemy in order to diminish the passions, and then be vigilant lest they increase once more. Again, fight to acquire the virtues and then be vigilant in order to keep them. This is the meaning of 'cultivating' and 'keeping' (cf. Gen. 2:15)."
– **St. Maximos the Confessor**

Maximos was in Rome during the height of the controversy over the nature and will of Christ. The newly elected Pope Martin I convened a council attended by 105 bishops who condemned monothelitism, the view that Christ possessed both divine and human natures but only divine will. It was a bold move given the emperor's support of the Monothelite doctrine. The emperor ordered the arrest of both Pope Martin and Maximos, who may have authored the council's condemnation of monothelitism. Pope Martin was condemned without a trial but died before his sentence could be carried out. Maximos was returned to Constantinople and was tried for heresy in 658. Among the accusations against him was the claim that he aided the Muslims in their conquests in Egypt and North Africa, which Maximos denied vehemently. He was sent into exile for his refusal to repudiate the Dyothelite doctrine.

"When the intellect is stripped of passions and illuminated with the contemplation of created beings, then it can enter into God and pray as it should."
– **St. Maximos the Confessor**

In 662, four years after first being exiled, Maximos was once again tried for and convicted of heresy. His tongue was then mutilated to silence his voice against the view that Christ had only a divine will, though his nature was both divine and human. His right hand was also severed, so that he couldn't express his views in writing either. Soon after his exile and imprisonment in a fortress in what is now Georgia, Maximos died.

> "When the body dies, it is wholly separated from the things of this world. Similarly, when the intellect dies while in that supreme state of prayer, it is separated from all conceptual images of this world. If it does not die such a death, it cannot be with God and live with Him."
> – **St. Maximos the Confessor**

Shortly after Maximos died in 662, in present-day Georgia, the Third Council of Constantinople upheld his theology, which was based on the view that Christ has both human and divine natures and human and divine wills. Monothelitism was made heresy and Maximos was posthumously exonerated of all charges, as was Pope Martin I. Maximos was venerated as a saint shortly after his death. He bears the title "Confessor" because he suffered for his Christian faith through the mutilation of his tongue and right hand, though he was not directly martyred. He is also known as Maximos the Theologian and Maximos of Constantinople and is recognized as a Father of the Church.

> "I have my room, some books and a nearby chapel. That is complete happiness."
> – **St. Miguel of Ecuador**

Upon entering the Brothers of the Christian Schools, more commonly called the La Salle Brothers, Francisco Luis-Cordero y Munoz took the name Miguel. From his birth in Ecuador in 1854, he was disabled with no use of his legs. He was cured at age five when he received a vision of the Mother of God. The Brothers of the Christian Schools had recently opened its first school in Ecuador, which Francisco entered as a nine-year-old boy. In 1868, he became the first Ecuadoran to join the order and assumed the name "Miguel." Brother Miguel taught in Quito for more than 30 years, publishing several textbooks, some of which were adopted by the Ecuadoran government for nationwide use. He gained an international reputation as an educator and writer, while still conducting religious retreats and catechizing children.

"The heart is rich when it is content, and it is always content when its desires are fixed on God."
– **St. Miguel of Ecuador**

Brother Miguel never left Ecuador until he was sent to represent his order at the 1888 beatification of its founder, John Baptist de la Salle. In 1905 he would again travel to Europe, this time to Belgium, to translate French texts into Spanish. Three years later he was transferred to Barcelona and continued his work until his death in 1910 from pneumonia. After confirmation of a miraculous healing that occurred through his intercession in 1935, he was beatified in 1977. He was canonized in 1984 by Pope John Paul II after confirmation of another miraculous healing. St. Miguel of Ecuador is the patron of the Brothers of the Christian Schools.

> "Son, nothing in this world now affords me delight. I do not know what there is now left for me to do or why I am still here, all my hopes in this world being now fulfilled."
> – **St. Monica** (on her deathbed, to her son, St. Augustine of Hippo)

Born into a Christian family in North Africa in 331, Monica was given in marriage to a wealthy Roman pagan named Patricius. Though he didn't share her beliefs, he respected them. However, he would not permit their children to be baptized. It was one of the great joys of her life that through her prayers and example she successfully converted him, along with his short-tempered mother, a year before Patricius died. When Augustine rejected Christianity and became a Manichaean, she drove him from her home before a vision prompted her to reconcile with him. She spent 17 years trying to convert him, and with the help of St. Ambrose, she was able to do so. Augustine was baptized, and mother and son were on their way back to North Africa to spread the Word of God when Monica died. The words she shared with her son as she lay dying confirmed that she had accomplished her mission in life—bringing her loved ones into the Church. Her epitaph, written by St. Augustine, reads in part, "Serving the heavenly laws of peace, you taught the people entrusted to you with your character."

"Nothing is far from God."
– **St. Monica**

Monica, mother of St. Augustine of Hippo, was traveling with her sons, about to embark on a ship in the Roman seaport of Ostia to return home to Tagaste, North Africa (present-day Algeria) when she fell ill. Realizing that she was close to death, they asked her if she feared dying so far from home, as she had previously expressed her desire to be buried beside her husband in Tagaste. The words she uttered in response, "Nothing is far from God," were a simple expression of the deep faith that had sustained her throughout her life. St. Monica was buried at Ostia, where she died. Her relics are now in a chapel within the Basilica di Sant'Agostino in Rome, built to honor her son, St. Augustine of Hippo.

"The giver of every good and perfect gift has called upon us to mimic God's giving, by grace, through faith, and this is not of ourselves."
– **St. Nicholas of Myra**

St. Nicholas, who is believed to have lived from roughly 280 to 343, was born in what is now Turkey. Little is known for certain about his life other than that he lost both parents when he was a young man and used his inheritance to help those in need and that he served as bishop of Myra, now the city of Demre. His kindness and generosity gave rise to many legends from which the fictional Santa Claus evolved. One such legend describes how Nicholas came to the aid of a family that was so poor that the three daughters faced the prospect of having to prostitute themselves or face starvation if they didn't marry, and there was no money for dowries. When he heard of their plight, he tossed a bag of gold through the window one night, enabling the first daughter to marry. He did the same a second time, and the second daughter married. Each time, Nicholas was able to keep the source of the gift anonymous. The third time, however, the father saw Nicholas as he ran away, and the story of Nicholas' generous gifts spread quickly.

> "Unwittingly you have pursued falsehood thinking it to be the truth. If you had been taught the truth first you would have been found effortlessly tending toward salvation, just as you now effortlessly lean toward perdition."
> – **St. Norbert**, to the people of Antwerp

St. Norbert spent the second part of his life making up for the first part. He was born into wealth in the Rhineland around 1080. He indulged in earthly pleasures even after he entered the worldly German court, where he accepted holy orders as a canon to boost his status and gain financially, but he drew the line at becoming a priest. His life changed forever when he fell from a horse and lay unconscious in the rain for an hour. When he came to, he spoke aloud: "Lord, what do you want me to do?" The answer he heard in his heart was to "Turn from evil and do good. Seek peace and pursue it." Norbert returned to his hometown, prepared for the priesthood, and was ordained at the age of roughly 35. He gave all his possessions to the poor and became an itinerant preacher. He lived the remainder of his life in the strictest obedience to the will of God, forming a community of canons living under an ascetic regimen and advancing in the Church. Three attempts were made on his life for the reforms he tried to bring. He was appointed archbishop of Magdeburg shortly before his death in 1134. St. Norbert was canonized in 1582.

P

"I bind to myself today the power in the love of the Seraphim, in the obedience of the Angels, in the ministration of the Archangels, in the hope of Resurrection unto reward, in the prayers of the Patriarchs, in the predictions of the Prophets, in the preaching of the Apostles, in the faith of the Confessors, in the purity of the holy Virgins, in the deeds of Righteous men."
– **St. Patrick of Ireland**

St. Patrick of Ireland was not a native of Ireland. He was born in Roman Britannia and was captured, enslaved, and taken to Ireland at age 14 by Irish pirates. Patrick, a Christian, spent the next seven years among the Druids and pagans of Ireland until he escaped and made his way back to his family. He credited his escape to his guardian angel, Victor, who manifested in human form and told him to go the coast, where he found sympathetic sailors to take him back to Britannia. It was another vision of Victor that prompted him to enter the priesthood. After his ordination as a bishop, he was given the mission of converting the nonbelievers in Ireland. Legend has it that his success in converting the Irish was due to God's intervention with a Druid chieftain. Instead of killing Patrick as he had intended, the chieftain became a convert and supporter of Patrick's work. Patrick spent the next 40 years preaching all over Ireland, bringing people into the faith and building churches.

> "The Lord opened the understanding of my unbelieving heart so that I should recall my sins."
> **– St. Patrick of Ireland**

It is said that St. Patrick used the three-leafed shamrock to illustrate and explain the Holy Trinity to the Irish Druids and pagans he was converting to Christianity. He used the shamrock with its one stem and three leaves as an analogy for God as one spirit expressed in three ways. St. Patrick is also credited with ridding Ireland of all its snakes, though there is no evidence of there ever having been snakes in Ireland. Many other miracles are attributed to St. Patrick, who acknowledged in his writings some of the wonders God performed through him. Most notably, he is said to have resurrected 33 people, some of them long dead. He acknowledged these resurrections in a letter, stating "in the name of our Lord Jesus Christ, I have raised from the dead bodies that have been buried many years." Patrick died on March 17, 461, in the town where he had established his first Irish church.

"Let love be genuine; hate what is evil, hold fast to what is good; love one another with brotherly affection; outdo one another in showing honor. Never flag in zeal, be aglow with the Spirit, serve the Lord. Rejoice in your hope, be patient in tribulation, be constant in prayer. Contribute to the needs of the saints, practice hospitality."
– **St. Paul the Apostle to the Gentiles**, or Saul of Tarsus (Romans 12:9-13)

Paul is the Roman name of Saul of Tarsus who was born a Jew but inherited Roman citizenship from his father. He was educated in Jerusalem, but little else is known of his early life. His conversion on the road to Damascus is recounted in the Acts of the Apostles. A devout Jew in the Pharisaic tradition, he had a vision of the resurrected Jesus, who asked Saul why he had persecuted Him. When Saul asked, "Who art thou Lord," He answered, "I am Jesus, whom thou persecutest." After his vision, Saul was blinded for three days and had to be led into Damascus. During those three days he neither ate nor drank, praying the entire time. Ananias of Damascus came to Saul, laid his hands on him, and told him that the Lord had sent him so that Saul might see again and be filled with the Holy Spirit. Scales fell from Saul's eyes, and able to see again, he rose from his bed and was baptized.

"Whoever, therefore, eats the bread or drinks the cup of the Lord in an unworthy manner will be guilty of profaning the body and blood of the Lord. Let a man examine himself, and so eat of the bread and drink of the cup. For anyone who eats and drinks without discerning the body eats and drinks judgment upon himself."
– **St. Paul the Apostle to the Gentiles,** or Saul of Tarsus (1 Corinthians 11:27)

Following his conversion, Saul of Tarsus went into the synagogues and proclaimed Jesus the Son of God. Those present were astonished to hear these words from the man who had previously berated Jews for saying the very same thing and even had them dragged in front of the chief priests. Now known by his Roman name, Paul would himself be persecuted for spreading the Gospel, which he claimed to have received directly from Jesus. He made missionary journeys to convert Gentiles and found himself in opposition to Peter over the fact that the Gentile Christians in Antioch did not strictly adhere to Jewish customs. He later wrote of saying to Peter, "You are a Jew, yet you live like a Gentile and not like a Jew. How is it, then, that you force Gentiles to follow Jewish customs?" Another point of contention was whether Gentile converts needed to be circumcised. Ultimately, as the early Church grew, it became accepted that one did not need to embrace Judaism to be a follower of Jesus.

"Have this mind among yourselves, which was in Christ Jesus, who, though he was in the form of God, did not count equality with God a thing to be grasped, but emptied himself, taking the form of a servant, being born in the likeness of men. And being found in human form he humbled himself and became obedient unto death, even death on a cross. Therefore God has highly exalted him and bestowed on him the name which is above every name, that at the name of Jesus every knee should bow, in heaven and on earth and under the earth, and every tongue confess that Jesus Christ is Lord, to the glory of God the Father."
– **St. Paul the Apostle to the Gentiles**, or Saul of Tarsus
(Philippians 2:5-9)

Paul the Apostle was criticized by Jewish authorities for ostensibly telling Jews among the Gentiles he was converting to abandon Jewish law and customs. He experienced the same kind of persecution that before his conversion he had exercised against those who said that Jesus was the Son of God. He and his companions were imprisoned in Jerusalem and then sent to Rome for trial, where he spent another two years under house arrest, apparently preaching from his rented home. It is not known exactly how or when Paul died, though his death is believed to have occurred sometime between the Great Fire of Rome in the year 64 and the end of Nero's reign in 68. There are several historical accounts, most of which agree that Paul was martyred by beheading, but they differ in the details.

> "Keep interior peace at every cost; pay no attention to fears or scruples. Experience will teach you that those vain fears of sin, etc., which I call veritable follies, ought to disappear in the fire of love."
> **– St. Paul of the Cross**

At the age of 26, St. Paul of the Cross was divinely inspired to found a congregation in honor of the Passion of Jesus Christ. In a vision he saw the habit members of the congregation would wear, and he was vested with that habit by Bishop Gastinara of Alexandria in 1720. Today's Passionists wear the same habit. The first member to join Paul in his new community was his own brother, John Baptist. Neither of them had yet studied theology or been ordained. A few years after establishing the Congregation of Discalced Clerks of the Holy Cross and Passion of Our Lord for priests, Paul established one for nuns. He also built the first Passionist Retreat (the Passionist term for a monastery) near Obitello. For decades, Paul traveled all over Italy preaching on the Passion of Christ. On his travels, he always carried a large wooden crucifix, which is how he became known as Paul of the Cross.

"Know that one grain of pride suffices to overthrow a mountain of holiness. Be humble, then, and endeavor to know yourself."
– **St. Paul of the Cross**

St. Paul of the Cross lived an austere and penitent life, displaying his love of God and devotion to the Passion of Christ in everything he said and did. In more than half a century as an itinerant preacher, he went barefoot, no matter how harsh the weather or how rough the terrain. He never considered himself to be anything more than a humble servant and lowly sinner. The appeal of his message and the example of holiness he provided drew enormous crowds of people who followed him from town to town on his preaching missions throughout Italy. His own sacrifices and penances, along with numerous signs from heaven, caused countless others to repent and convert.

> "Prayer, good reading, the frequentation of the sacraments, with the proper dispositions, and particularly the flight of idleness - these are, believe me, the means of sanctifying yourself."
> **– St. Paul of the Cross**

St. Paul of the Cross credited his guardian angel for several miraculous events, including saving his life on more than one occasion. For example, one time he slipped while climbing a large rock and was supported safely by unseen hands while he regained his footing. On another occasion, he was unable to walk another step, half-frozen in extremely cold weather, when he was lifted into the air and carried a great distance by an angel, his feet only touching ground when he was within a few steps of his destination. Paul also confided in a friend that on several occasions, when he was standing in front of crowds to preach, ill health prevented him from saying a word, and his guardian angel took his shape and preached in his place. One story that's often recounted is that of a man who finally went to confession after 50 years of living in sacrilege because he said Father Paul waved a sword at him and threatened to kill him if he didn't repent. Father Paul was nowhere in the vicinity at the time, and when asked by a fellow priest about his new way of getting people to go to confession, he told him that it was his guardian angel who had taken Father Paul's shape and acted on his behalf, as he had done on other occasions.

"When you feel the assaults of passion and anger, then is the time to be silent as Jesus was silent in the midst of His ignominies and sufferings."
– **St. Paul of the Cross**

Paul of the Cross was born Paolo Francesco Danei in 1694, in the town of Ovada in northern Italy. He received his early education at a boarding school for boys operated by a priest and returned home at age 15. At 19, while helping his father in the family business, he developed a lifelong devotion to the Passion of Christ. At 21 he left to join a crusade to defend the Venetian Republic against the Turks, but he quickly decided he was being called to another kind of life. It was not until 1727, several years after founding the Passionists, that Paul and his brother, John Baptist, were ordained as priests and devoted themselves to preaching missions in parishes. When they established their first Retreat a decade later, there were nine members of the Passionist community. The Passionist life was an austere one that emphasized solitude and contemplation, with at least three hours devoted to contemplative prayer every day. This is what Paul believed was necessary for those preaching about the Passion of Christ. After nearly fifty years of preaching all over Italy, Paul of the Cross died in Rome at the age of 81. Nearly a century later he was canonized by Pope Pius IX in 1867.

> "Live in the joy and the peace of the divine Majesty. Live lost in divine love. Live for divine love and of divine love."
> **– St. Paul of the Cross**

Several miracles that occurred after his death were attributed to St. Paul of the Cross. Even as his body lay in the church before burial, a girl was cured of a painful ulcer in her cheek by kissing his hand and touching her cheek to it. The cure was instantaneous and witnessed by the crowd that was present. In December of 1776, the year following Paul's death, holding a picture of him to an infant with serious deformities produced a miraculous cure. One of the miracles for beatification was the 1816 cure of a surgeon's seven-year old son who was believed by several physicians to be close to death. The father suddenly remembered that he had a scrap Father Paul's habit in the house. He ran to get it, moistened it with water, and placed in the senseless, unmoving boy's mouth, and within moments he sat up and asked for food, completely well. The other miracle for beatification was the 1844 cure of a woman suffering from breast cancer who wore a scrap of Father Paul's habit on her breast, beneath her clothing, prayed for several days, and was completely cured. These are but a few examples of the many healing miracles experienced by people who touched bits of Father Paul's habit or artifacts he had used in life or who simply prayed for his intercession.

"Having arrived at this moment of my existence, I believe that no one of you thinks I want to hide the truth. That is why I declare to you that there is no other way of salvation than the one followed by Christians. Since this way teaches me to forgive my enemies and all who have offended me, I willingly forgive the king and all those who have desired my death. And I pray that they will obtain the desire of Christian baptism."
– **St. Paul Miki** (one of the Martyrs of Nagasaki)

On February 5, 1597, twenty-six Catholics were rounded up in Kyoto and Osaka during a persecution of Christians and forced to walk 800 km to Nagasaki to be crucified. Before they were crucified, the martyrs were mutilated by having their left ears cut off as a sign of disrespect. The twenty-six martyrs included six Spanish Franciscans, three Japanese Jesuits, 17 Japanese and Korean catechists, and three Japanese Jesuits. One of the Japanese Jesuits was Paul Miki, born into a wealthy, noble family as the son of a Japanese military leader. His family converted to Catholicism when Paul was a small boy, and he was baptized at the age of five. He was educated by the Jesuits and joined the Society of Jesus in 1580 when he was 22 years old. At the time of his martyrdom he was a novice, yet he led his fellow martyrs in prayer and encouraged them as they awaited the spear that would soon be thrust into the side of each. From his cross, he forgave the king and thanked God for allowing him to die for his faith. All the men and boys who were crucified that day were canonized in 1862 as the Martyrs of Japan, also known as the Martyrs of Nagasaki.

"The only reason for my being killed is that I have taught the doctrine of Christ. Thank God it is for this reason that I die."
– **St. Paul Miki** (one of the Martyrs of Nagasaki)

The persecution that resulted in the death by crucifixion of Paul Miki, a Japanese Jesuit novice and 25 other Catholic men and boys in Nagasaki in 1597 was part of a larger war on Christianity that took the lives of thousands of Catholics in Japan between 1597 and 1873. St. Francis Xavier brought the faith to Japan in 1549, and it flourished for nearly half a century. However, many in the government feared that missionaries would eventually be followed by soldiers intent on conquering Japan. In 1587, Christianity was banned, and all Christians were ordered to leave the country within 20 days. The ban was never actually enforced, and for the next ten years, both Jesuit and the more recently arrived Franciscans continued their work. Tensions grew between the Jesuits, who exercised discretion, and the Franciscans who preached and baptized converts in public. The trigger event for the martyrdom of Paul Miki and his companions was a Spanish ship captain's attempt to save his cargo from being confiscated. He pointed out on a map the vastness of the Spanish empire, which the Japanese interpreted as a threat of invasion. A second group martyrdom took place a few years later, taking the lives of 36 Jesuits, 26 Franciscans, 21 Dominicans, 5 Augustinians, and 107 lay people—men, women, and children. Collectively, these two groups, are referred to as the Martyrs of Japan, with St. Paul Miki's group known separately as the Martyrs of Nagasaki.

"Our Lord wills that you cling to Him alone! If your faith were greater how much more peaceful you would be even when great trials surround and oppress you."
– **St. Paula Frassinetti**

Paula (Paola in Italian) was born in Genoa in 1809, was baptized the same day, and had a happy life until her mother died nine years later. Her death left Paula to manage the household and care for her four brothers, all of whom went on to become priests. She was particularly close to her older brother, Giuseppi, who had long conversations with her about faith. Paula thought she, too, might be called to religious life, but her father would not hear of it. She was needed at home, and there she remained until she was 19, when she needed a break and went to stay with her brother, Father Giuseppe, who was a parish priest in Genoa. Helping him in his work with the poor children of the parish, she realized she had a talent for teaching. She also began thinking about living in community with other like-minded women, and in 1934, she started to do so with six other young women. They worked for pay to earn money to use in educating children from very poor families, believing that the way to bring them to God was to educate them. This was the beginning of the Sisters of St. Dorothy, which grew and expanded to other countries. Her legacy continues today as Sisters of St. Dorothy are teaching on five continents. St. Paula Frassinetti was canonized nearly a century later in 1984.

"It is most certain that the malice of our own hearts is the principal cause that hinders us from attaining to our beatitude and everlasting happiness, because it makes us slow to godly actions, dull to virtuous exercises, and suggests a greater difficulty in them than there is, which if it were not a man might walk without any molestation in the way of virtue, and at length without labor attain to his desired end."
– **St. Peter of Alcantara**

St. Peter of Alcantara led a life of great austerity and penitence from the moment he became a Franciscan Friar of the Stricter Observance at the young age of 16. His abilities were quickly recognized, and he was already superior of a new house before he was even ordained as a priest. It was a time of great Church reform, and Peter's insistence on strict rules and demanding penance inspired many. In 1114, Peter established the Alcantarines, a group of Franciscans who followed the Rule of St. Francis even more rigorously than the Franciscan Friars of the Stricter Observance did. (Eventually, the Alcantarines merged with other Observant friars to become the Order of Friars Minor.) While serving as confessor and spiritual director to St. Theresa of Avila, Peter encouraged her efforts to bring reform to the Poor Clares.

> "Blissful penance, which has purchased for me so great a reward!"
> – **St. Peter of Alcantara,** to St. Teresa of Avila, appearing to her after his death

Much of what is known about St. Peter of Alcantara comes from the writings of St. Teresa of Avila. She had other spiritual directors before Peter, but none seemed to understand her mystical experiences. She described his severe penitential practices, which she believed helped make him a "very holy and spiritual man." He ate very little, sometimes going three days or even a week without food, and he slept only 90 minutes a night. Observers at the time who described his death noted that he prayed on his knees and refused water when it was offered to him, because Christ thirsted on the cross and Peter deserved no better. He was praying at the moment of his death in 1562. He was canonized in 1669.

> "To love God as He ought to be loved, we must be detached from all temporal love. We must love nothing but Him, or if we love anything else, we must love it only for His sake."
> – **St. Peter Claver**

Cartagena was one of two ports where slaves from Africa arrived to be sold in South America. Between the years 1616 and 1650, Peter Claver worked daily to minister to the needs of the 10,000 slaves who arrived each year. As each ship arrived with a cargo of slaves from Africa, Peter ministered to their physical and spiritual needs. Accompanied by a translator, he boarded the ship while the slaves were still imprisoned in the hold and gave them fresh fruit and other food donated by sympathetic Cartagenians. Once the slaves were locked up in holding pens in the city, Peter continued his work with them. With the help of his translator, he provided rudimentary medical care, taught the slaves the basics of Catholicism, and baptized as many of them as possible. He knew that slave owners would treat baptized slaves more humanely than non-Christian slaves, especially if Peter appealed to their conscience. During the off-season, when few ships made the crossing from Africa, Peter traveled from plantation to plantation, continuing to minister to the slaves and ensuring that they weren't being mistreated. By the time he became sick and unable to carry on his work in 1651, Peter had baptized more than 300,000 slaves.

> "We must speak to them with our hands before we speak to them with our lips."
> **– St. Peter Claver**

Peter Claver never returned to his native Spain after 34 years of ministering to the slaves arriving in Cartagena, Colombia from Africa. During the last three years of his life, he was too ill to leave his room or even his bed. Ironically, the former slave engaged to care for Peter treated him very badly, though Peter never complained about being left without food and going unbathed. In fact, he believed that he deserved to suffer for his sins. The people of Cartagena were deeply saddened by the news that Peter was close to death, and many flocked to his home to see him one last time. He was regarded as being holy and saintly in life, and his admirers stripped his room of anything that could serve as a relic. At his 1888 canonization, Pope Leo XIII declared that no life other than Christ's had ever moved him as much as he had been moved by the life of St. Peter Claver, and in 1896, he named Peter the patron of missionary work among all African peoples.

"Fasting is the soul of prayer, mercy is the lifeblood of fasting. So if you pray, fast; if you fast, show mercy; if you want your petition to be heard, hear the petition of others. If you do not close your ear to others, you open God's ear to yourself."
– **St. Peter Chrysologus**

Fifth century Bishop Peter of Ravenna is perhaps best known for his homilies, a form of sermon he pioneered out of his aversion to boring his listeners. His short, simple inspiration messages earned him the title "Doctor of Homilies." The Roman Empress Galla Placidia dubbed him *Chrysologus*, which means "golden-worded," upon hearing the first homily he delivered after being appointed bishop in 433. St. Peter Chrysologus died in his home town, Imola, Italy, in 450 at the age of 44. He was made a Doctor of the Church in 1729, largely because of his homilies on Gospel subjects, most of which have survived the centuries.

> "The hermit's cell is the meeting-place of God and man, a cross-roads for those who dwell in the flesh and heavenly things. For there the citizens of heaven hold intercourse with men, not in the language of the flesh, but by being made manifest, without any clamour of tongues, to the rich and secret places of the soul."
> – **St. Peter Damian**

Peter, born in Ravenna, Italy in 1007, was orphaned as a young child and was taken in by an older brother who treated the boy like a slave and assigned him to tending the pigs. Another brother, the archpriest of Ravenna, stepped in and served as surrogate father to Peter. He sent Peter to good schools and encouraged him in his studies. Peter took this brother's name, Damian, as his own surname. Peter excelled as a scholar and became a respected professor. Even as a student, Peter lived an austere life to prevent himself from falling into sinful ways. Fasting, watching, prayer, and the physical discomfort of the hair shirt he wore beneath his clothes led him to desire a life of even greater discipline and holiness. Already contemplating a monastic life, he was receptive to the message of two Benedictines he met by chance, and what they told him about their Rule and the way they lived prompted him to join their hermitage. As a hermit, he immersed himself in sacred studies and became the abbot's chosen successor, which Peter agreed to only after the abbot made it a matter of obedience. Upon the abbot's death around 1043, Peter governed the community with wisdom and piety and founded five more hermitages over the years.

> "As the soul is the life of the body, so the Holy Spirit is the life of our souls."
> – **St. Peter Damian**

St. Peter Damian would have been content to spend his entire life within the walls of the hermitage he governed as abbot from the time of the former abbot's death in 1043, when Peter was in his mid-forties. His main responsibility, as he saw it, was to ensure the development of a spirit of solitude, charity, and humility among the members of his community and the five hermitages he founded. But his talents as a negotiator and peacemaker were in great demand by the Popes who reigned during his lifetime. In 1057, Pope Stephen IX prevailed upon Peter to leave his hermitage and become Cardinal-bishop of Ostia, but Peter's longing for solitude was powerful. He petitioned Stephen's successor, Nicholas II, to let him retire from his bishopric, but it was Nicholas' successor, Alexander II, who reluctantly agreed to let Peter return to monastic life with one stipulation—that he could call Peter back if his services were needed. Peter did not return to supervising the communities under his control, living instead as a simple monk.

"For the wisdom of the flesh brings death, but that of the spirit brings life and peace, since the wisdom of the flesh is the enemy of God; it is not subject to God's law, nor can it be. And since the wisdom of the flesh is unable to bear the yoke of God's law, it cannot look upon it either, for its eyes are clouded with the smoke of pride."
– **St. Peter Damian**

St. Peter Damian was nearly as active in his retirement as a monk as he was during his years as Cardinal-bishop of Ostia. He wrote prolifically, often sending written rebukes to clergy and Church officials for what he saw as spiritual laxity in the performance of their duties or insufficient discipline in their own lives. For example, he chastised the Bishop of Florence for playing a game of chess and the Bishop of Besancon for allowing the Canons of his church to sing the Divine Office while seated rather than standing. He weighed in against monks traveling abroad and not adhering firmly enough to their vow of poverty and insisted on clerical celibacy. Vehement in his insistence on primitive discipline, he was as strict with himself as he was with others, but he was also quick to praise when he thought it was deserved. Pope Alexander II continued to call on Peter to represent the Church in important matters, such as prevailing on Henry IV, the king of Germany, not to persist in his efforts to obtain a divorce. His last mission for the Church was to travel to Ravenna to deal with its recently excommunicated archbishop and his accomplices in his crimes, though Archbishop Henry died before Peter arrived. Peter was on his way back from Ravenna when he fell ill and died in 1072. He was declared a Doctor of the Church in 1828.

> "Keep your soul at peace, in order to be able to be attentive and very faithful to the inner movement of the Holy Spirit."
> **– St. Peter Julian Eymard**

Peter Julian Eymard was born on February 4, 1811, in La Mure, France. He grew up in a poor family in Europe after the French Revolution, a time when Catholicism was not looked upon kindly.

His interest in pursuing a religious life was apparent from a very early age. One of the most often repeated stories about him tells of an event that occurred when he was about five. He disappeared from home while his sister was caring for him, triggering a frantic search that eventually took her to the village church. Peter had dragged a small ladder over to the tabernacle and was standing on it with his ear pressed against the door. When his sister asked what he was doing he said, "Listening to Jesus. I can hear him better this way." As a child, Peter wrote several prayers for different occasions, including this one to be recited after communion: "My dear Jesus, I thank you for the grace which you have given me that you have come to dwell in my heart." When Peter first told his father of his desire to become a priest, his father was opposed to the idea as Peter was his only surviving son. When Peter did go to seminary, he became seriously ill and was sent home. He tried again after his father's death and was ordained as a priest for the Diocese of Grenoble in 1834, when he was 23 years old.

> "He loves, He hopes, He waits. If He came down on our altars on certain days only, some sinner, on being moved to repentance, might have to look for Him, and not finding Him, might have to wait. Our Lord prefers to wait Himself for the sinner for years rather than keep him waiting one instant."
> **– St. Peter Julian Eymard**

Peter Julian Eymard started out his ecclesiastical career as a parish priest in 1834 when he joined the Society of Mary and became the Marist's provincial in Lyon. A growing interest in the Eucharist led him to leave the Marists and establish the Congregation of the Blessed Sacrament in 1856, evangelizing among the young and poor workers of Paris. One of his goals was to get lay people actively involved in the life of the Church. The members of the congregation prayed before and guarded the Blessed Sacrament around the clock. The congregation was very poor and had trouble providing consistent food and shelter, which made it hard to attract members, but it continued to grow. Though Father Eymard was in poor health during his later years, he helped Marguerite Guillot, one of the women who came to him for spiritual direction, establish the Sister Servants of the Blessed Sacrament. By the time Father Eymard died in 1868, he had helped many clergy and lay people rediscover the Eucharist.

> "It costs little to tell God we love Him when He is showering favors upon us; it is in the midst of the tempest that we must cry out to Him like Job: "Although He should kill me, I will trust Him."
> – **St. Peter Julian Eymard**

The world might never have known such famed sculptures as Auguste Rodin's "The Thinker" if it hadn't been for the intervention of St. Peter Julian Eymard. In 1862 Rodin was anguished by the death of his older sister Maria from peritonitis. Maria had entered a convent after being spurned by an unfaithful suitor—a man introduced to her by Auguste. In his grief, Auguste joined the Congregation of the Blessed Sacrament founded by Father Eymard. It didn't take long for Eymard, the head of the Congregation, to recognize Rodin's talent and his lack of suitability for religious life. Eymard encouraged Rodin to return to his sculpting and allowed him to use the congregation's garden shed as a studio. One of Rodin's first works was a bust of Father Eymard. After five months in the Congregation, Rodin left and continued his training as a sculptor. A 2017 article quotes Father Eymard as saying to Rodin: "Draw, model, trim, shape... and give the world your soul through Beauty. I am a priest and I do not know how to do it... Some pray and save another person. Others paint, build or sculpt and make others better. Some are roots, others trunks and then there are all those who are branches, leaves, flowers and fruits."

"Hear Mass daily; it will prosper the whole day. All your duties will be performed the better for it, and your soul will be stronger to bear its daily cross. The Mass is the most holy act of religion; you can do nothing that can give greater glory to God or be more profitable for your soul than to hear Mass both frequently and devoutly. It is the favorite devotion of the saints."
– St. Peter Julian Eymard

Eymard's 1962 canonization was later described by the Superior-General of the Blessed Sacrament Congregation as "the most extraordinary of all canonisations in the history of the Church by reason of the attendance of so many cardinals and bishops." The reason that about 60 cardinals and more than 2,000 bishops attended the three-hour ceremony was that the first session of the Second Vatican Council had just ended, and the attendees were all still in Rome. It was actually a triple canonization, as two contemporaries of Eymard— Anthony Mary Pucci (a Servite priest) and Francis Mary of Camporosso (a Capuchin lay brother)—were canonized by Pope John XXIII during the same ceremony. St. Peter Julian Eymard is often referred to as the "Apostle of the Eucharist."

> "In visiting the dying we should not say many words to them, but rather help them by praying for them."
> – **St. Philip Neri**

Life doesn't always unfold the way we expect it to, and that was certainly the case for Philip Neri, born in 1515 in Florence, Italy. Though he received his early education from the Dominican friars in San Marco, he appeared to be headed for a secular career. At 18, he went to San Germano to live with a wealthy family member to work in and eventually inherit the family business. But he had barely gotten settled in when he had a mystical encounter with the Lord that he interpreted as a call to religious life—a call that took him to Rome. In Rome, Philip took a position as live-in tutor in the household of another Florentine. When he was not teaching and counseling his two young charges, he kept to himself and lived an ascetic life, consuming little more than bread and water and spending much time in prayer. He began his studies in theology and philosophy, but after three years, he felt no call to become ordained. Rather, he acted on his desire to help the poor and bring Romans back to the Church.

> "When a man knows how to break down his own will and to deny his soul what it desires, he has got a good degree in virtue."
> **– St. Philip Neri**

Philip Neri had a way with people. He had a knack for striking up conversations and engaging people in discussion wherever he was—on street corners and in public squares, wherever people gathered. He had a pleasant personality and a great sense of humor, and he listened as well as he spoke. People listened to Philip as well, following his lead into service to the poor and sick and into a relationship with Jesus Christ. He evangelized all over Rome, sharing the Gospel and bringing people into, or back to, the Church. That was Philip's life by day. His nights were spent praying alone in the church or in the city's ancient catacombs. In 1548, Philip established a confraternity of laymen, poor themselves, to serve the poor and participate in spiritual exercises. He moved easily among people of all walks of life and developed friendships with Ignatius of Loyola, Charles Borromeo, Pius V, and others of great faith and influence.

> "We must pray incessantly for the gift of perseverance."
> – **St. Philip Neri**

Philip Neri's confessor, who helped him found a confraternity of laymen, finally convinced him that he would be even more effective in his work if he became ordained as a priest, which he finally did when he was 36. He joined the other priests living at San Girolamo where he spent long hours in the confessional, listening and talking to people much as he had while evangelizing on the streets of Rome. So many people came seeking his advice and spiritual counsel that a large room was added to the church to accommodate the crowds. Other priests joined Philip in this "oratory," and they became known collectively as the "Oratorians." It would be a few years before the Congregation of the Priests of the Oratory was founded with the mission of helping people develop spiritually. The Congregation was officially approved in 1575 when Philip Neri was 60 years old.

"Without mortification nothing can be done."
– **St. Philip Neri**

Philip Neri came to be known as the Apostle of Rome during his later years in recognition of his decades of work bringing lay people into more active involvement in the Church, which had fallen into clericalism. As Philip saw it, far too many clergy spent their time with other clergy and had only minimal contact with the lay people of Rome. Philip, on the other hand, maintained an "open door" policy and was always surrounded by people. Even as his health deteriorated, he was always available to hear their confessions, join people in prayer, and minister to their spiritual needs. Though church and secular leaders relied on him for advice, his first obligation was always to the poor. No one in Rome was better loved or respected than father Neri.

> "He who always acts under obedience may be assured that he will not have to give an account of his actions to God."
> **– St. Philip Neri**

Philip Neri's health had been slowly declining for a decade when, in 1595, on the Feast of Corpus Christi, his physician told him that he was not well. Realizing that the end was near, Philip maintained his usual routine of hearing confessions and receiving visitors. Taking his leave for the night, Philip said, "Last of all, we must die," and went to bed. He died around midnight, at the age of 80. St. Philip Neri was canonized by Pope Gregory XV in 1622 and is the patron of Rome, the U.S. Special Forces, and of humor and joy.

> "Our Lord loves you and loves you tenderly; and if He does not let you feel the sweetness of His love, it is to make you more humble and abject in your own eyes."
> – **St. Pio**

By the time Francesco Forgione, born in Pietrelcina, Italy in 1887, was five years old, he had decided to dedicate his life to God. He attended Mass every day with his parents and siblings and was an altar server in the parish church. Though his parents were religious and supportive of their son's desire to serve God, they were poor farmers and needed Francesco's help. Responsible for tending the family's sheep and frequently ill, he attended school only sporadically and fell behind his peers. By the age of ten, he had completed only three years of school and was told when he applied to become a friar in a nearby community of monks that he lacked the necessary education. To pay the cost of a private tutor, Francesco's father sailed to America and sent money home. At 15, Francisco met the requirements to enter the novitiate of the Capuchin friars in Morcone, taking the name Pio, in honor of Pope Pius I. Unfortunately, serious illness forced him to leave the novitiate and return home, though he continued his studies and preparation for the priesthood.

"Pray, Hope, and Don't Worry"
– St. Pio

Padre Pio suffered numerous medical problems throughout his life. He was ordained as a priest in 1910 but remained at home due to his frail health. A few years later, he joined a small agricultural community of brothers, Our Lady of Grace Capuchin Friary in the mountain town of San Giovani Rotondo, bringing the number of friars there to seven. He was drafted into the Italian Army during World War I but was sent home so often because of illness that he was discharged for medical reasons once and for all after 182 days of service. He returned to the friary where he would spend the rest of his life preaching, providing spiritual direction, and teaching in the seminary.

> "Fear not because God is with you."
> – **St. Pio**

From childhood, Padre Pio had mystical experiences that set him apart from his peers. He reportedly saw guardian angels and spoke with both Jesus and the Virgin Mary. As a young child, he assumed that everyone saw what he saw. He had episodes of ecstasy while praying, and during one of them, according to a fellow monk, he levitated. But what really drew attention to him was the appearance of stigmata on his hands and feet. The wounds were painful but smelled of roses and never became infected. According to the doctors who examined them, the stigmata were perfectly round. He bore his stigmata for the remainder of his life. By 1919, people were coming from far and wide to examine Padre Pio. It was an uncomfortable situation, not only for Padre Pio, who typically wore red or black gloves to conceal the stigmata on his hands when they were bleeding, but also for the Church. The Vatican took steps to keep him out of the public eye and ordered an investigation, which concluded that his stigmata were authentic.

> "We must know how to confide. There is the fear of God and the fear of a Judas. Too much fear makes one labour without love, and too much confidence prevents from considering the danger which we must overcome."
> **– St. Pio**

Though the Vatican originally restricted Padre Pio's interactions with the public after his stigmata and supernatural experiences attracted widespread attention, in 1934 those restrictions were removed, and Padre Pio was once again allowed to preach. Pope Pius XI went so far as to encourage people to visit him. In 1947, when Father Karol Wojtyla went to see Padre Pio, Pio told him that he would one day become pope—a prophecy that was realized in 1978 when Father Karol became Pope John Paul II. Padre Pio's rekindled popularity enabled him to raise funds to build a hospital in 1956, in the village of San Giovanni Rotondo, where he had been living in the friary for most of his adult life. When Pope Paul VI reviewed Padre Pio's case and dismissed any concerns about the authenticity of his stigmata, Pio's name became known around the world.

> "The life of a Christian is nothing but a perpetual struggle against self; there is no flowering of the soul to the beauty of its perfection except at the price of pain"
> – **St. Pio**

Padre Pio's health situation had been precarious for most of his life. In childhood he suffered bouts of gastroenteritis, typhoid fever, and many illnesses that were never specifically identified. Though he was cured of cancer after only two radiological treatments, he had numerous other health issues that persisted. He died in 1968, and over 100,000 people came to his funeral. St. Pio was canonized in 2002 by Pope John Paul II and is the patron of civil defense volunteers, adolescents, and the village of his birth, Pietrelcina, Italy. In 2008, St. Pio's body was exhumed, was prepared for display, and was placed in a crystal, marble, and silver sepulcher in the crypt of the monastery at San Giovanni Rotondo. The body was to remain on display until December 2008, but Church officials had to extend the viewing period to September 2009 to accommodate the more than 800,000 pilgrims who made reservations to view the remains of St. Pio.

"You are the salt of the earth! You are the light of the world! See to it that the people are edified by your example, by the purity of your lives, by the moderation of your conduct, and the brilliance of your holiness! God does not ask of you mere ordinary virtue. He demands downright perfection!"
– **Pope St. Pius V,** to the cardinals

Pope Pius V began his religious life as a Dominican friar, rose through the ranks of the Church, and headed it from 1566-1572. He is called "The Pope of the Rosary" for his great devotion to the Blessed Virgin Mary and promotion of the Holy Rosary. Specifically, he wrote a papal bull establishing standards for praying the Holy Rosary and established the feast of Our Lady of the Holy Rosary—a feast of Thanksgiving for the victory of the Christian fleet over that of the Ottoman Turks during the Battle of Lepanto in 1571. Pope Pius V had issued his papal bull two years before the battle for all of Europe to pray the Holy Rosary as instructed in that declaration. On the day of the Battle of Lepanto, he ordered a 40-hour devotion to the Blessed Virgin Mary, and he attributed the Christian victory to her intercession. Though far greater in number than the Christian fleet, all but a few of the nearly 300 Turkish ships sank or were captured, stopping further incursion by the Ottoman Turks.

> "We have nothing to say which you have not already heard, no doctrine to propound that is new to anyone; but we treat of matters which it is necessary for everyone to bear in mind, and God inspires us with the hope that our message will not fail to bear abundant fruit."
> **– Pope St. Pius X**

The last will and testament of Pope St. Pius X includes one sentence that illustrates his humility of heart: "I was born poor, I have lived in poverty, and I wish to die poor." The same quality is recognized in the epitaph inscribed on his tomb in the crypt of the basilica of St. Peter: "Born poor and humble of heart, Undaunted champion of the Catholic faith, Zealous to restore all things in Christ, Crowned a holy life with a holy death." Pius X, born Giuseppe Melchiorre Sarto on June 2 in 1835 in a small town, was the eldest of the eight surviving children of a cobbler and a seamstress of very modest means. Fortunately, young Giuseppe's intelligence, character, and academic performance in the parish school impressed the local pastor who arranged a scholarship for him to attend high school, and a few years later, he received another scholarship for the seminary in Padua. Father Sarto was ordained in 1858 at the age of 23.

> "If the Angels could envy, they would envy us for Holy Communion."
> **– Pope St. Pius X**

Father Sarto, the future Pope St. Pius X, began his ecclesiastical career as a curate in the parish of Tombolo, where he spent eight years working tirelessly with the poor, setting up a night school for adults, and training the parish choir. His pastor wrote these prophetic words about Father Sarto: "They have sent me as curate a young priest, with orders to mold him to the duties of pastor; in fact, however, the contrary is true. He is so zealous, so full of good sense, and other precious gifts that it is I who can learn much from him. Some day or other he will wear the mitre, of that I am sure. After that—who knows?"

"Holy Communion is the shortest and safest way to Heaven."
– **Pope St. Pius X**

When Sarto became Bishop of Mantua in 1884, anti-Church sentiment among secular authorities had created a laxity among clergy, especially younger priests, and seminary enrollment had plummeted. Such problems affected the laity as well, spreading religious indifference and secularism. Bishop Sarto sought to remedy the situation and reform the diocese, beginning with the example of his own zealous teaching to energize the clergy. When he became Cardinal and Patriarch of Venice in 1893, he continued to put great emphasis on the development of clergy, the education of the young, and help for the poor. He supported the newly formed Workingmen's Society and saved the diocesan newspaper from bankruptcy. He saw spiritual problems and social and economic problems as inextricably intertwined. Sarto was, much to his surprise, elected after the death of Leo XIII and became Pope Pius X in 1903.

"God being infinite beauty, the soul united to Christ draws upon himself the admiring and tender gaze of the Angels, who, were they capable of any passion, would be filled with envy at his lot."
– **Pope St. Pius X**

Pope Pius X announced that the aim of his papacy was to "restore all things in Christ." The two means to accomplish this restoration were things he had emphasized throughout his career: development of a trained and disciplined clergy and the religious instruction of young and old. He also instituted important reforms regarding Holy Communion, which earned him the nickname, "The Pope of the Eucharist." He instituted several reforms to promote Catholic social action, maintaining that prayer alone would not Christianize society, but he is perhaps best known for his vigorous opposition to Modernism, which he believed would destroy the foundation of faith. Pius X died of influenza shortly after the outbreak of World War I, and the humble parish priest was canonized in 1954.

> Charity is that with which no man is lost, and without which no man is saved.
> **– St. Robert Bellarmine**

When Pope Clementine VIII made Robert Bellarmine a cardinal, he said it was because Bellarmine was unequalled as a scholar. Born in Montepulciano, Italy in 1542, Robert Bellarmine entered the Society of Jesus at age 18, was ordained, and spent the next couple of decades teaching and writing before becoming Provincial of Naples in 1594 and Cardinal in 1598. He continued his scholarly activities in his austere quarters in the Vatican, expounding on subjects that tended to stir up controversy. He not only provided evidence as to why the theory of the divine right of kings was untenable, but also theorized that the pope had indirect power over temporal affairs, which made Bellarmine rather unpopular among royalty. In 1616, Bellarmine was required to deliver an admonition on behalf of the Holy Office to his friend, Galileo, for his support of the Copernican theory of a sun-centered solar system. Cardinal Robert Bellarmine died in 1621 but because of the controversial nature of some of his writings, he was not canonized until 1930—more than 300 years after the process was initiated. He was named a Doctor of the Church the following year.

"Where sin was hatched, let tears now wash the nest."
– **St. Robert Southwell**

St. Robert Southwell is one of the Forty Martyrs of England and Wales who were unjustly executed for treason between 1535 and 1679. The statute of 1585 had made it an act of treason to be a Catholic priest and administer the sacraments in England. Southwell was born in England, educated and ordained in Italy, and came back to England when he was 25, the year after the statute was enacted, knowing that his work as a priest would have to be clandestine. He escaped English authorities for six years until he was arrested in 1592 and held prisoner until he was tried on February 20, 1595 and sentenced to death. He was martyred the next day, at the age of 33, by hanging, drawing, and quartering. St. Robert Southwell was canonized in 1970, along with the 39 other martyrs of England and Wales, by Pope Paul VI.

"After prayer, on working days, I must go presently about some work or exercise that may be of some profit, and of all other things take heed of idleness, the mother of all vices. Towards eleven (if company and other more weighty causes will permit) I may meditate a little and call to mind how I have spent the morning, asking God grace to spend the afternoon better."
– **St. Robert Southwell** (from his handbook, *A Short Rule*)

St. Robert Southwell was not only a Jesuit priest and one of the Forty Martyrs of England and Wales, but he was also a talented poet and writer. Literary scholars identify Southwell as one of the influences on the work of William Shakespeare. He wrote prolifically during his six years as an underground Jesuit priest in London after the statute of 1585 made it treasonous to be a Catholic priest and administer the sacraments. In Southwell's time, his writing was very popular. He *wrote A Short Rule* to provide guidelines for laypeople trying to lead devout lives. The principles he espoused were based on the principles of religious life in monasteries and convents.

"Judge! I cannot give up my God. He is the Creator and Father to all of us. He loves virtue and punishes sin, so how could I abandon Him? Harming others is also a sin. A long time ago I decided to shed my blood for these truths. Do as you please."
– **St. Rosa Kim**

Kim Rosa was a 55-year old Korean convert to Catholicism when Cho-Pyong-ku took control of the Korean government. He hated Catholicism, which had already been banned by the king, and within a month he issued a decree to eliminate Catholicism from Korea. Kim Rosa and eight other Catholics already imprisoned because of their faith became the first victims of the purge. In 1838, the year before Cho Pyong-ku issued his edict, Kim Rosa was arrested in the middle of the night, dragged from her home by the police, and thrown into prison. She did not waver in her faith, even when the instruments of torture that would be used on her if she continued in her refusal to deny her God or to reveal the names of other Catholics were displayed in front of her. The judge had her tortured and then sentenced her to death. The sentence was not carried out until July 20, 1839, two weeks after Cho-Pyong-ku issued his edict to destroy Catholicism in Korea. Kim Rosa was canonized in 1984 in Seoul, Korea by Pope John Paul II.

> "The more I reflect on the graces I have received, the more they astonish me and make me tremble."
> – **St. Rose Philippine Duchesne**

St. Rose Philippine Duchesne, a French-born sister of the Society of the Sacred Heart, was known by the Native Americans she served as "the woman who is always praying." Born in Grenoble, France in 1769, it wasn't until 1818 that she realized her longstanding desire to do missionary work among the American Indians. Though originally invited to evangelize among and educate the Indian and French children in the New Orleans area, she and the four sisters who accompanied her ended up in Missouri, in what Sister Rose described as the "the remotest village in the U.S." where they started a new Sacred Heart convent in a log cabin. Within a decade, the Society of the Sacred Heart had six communities in the United States and operated several schools. In 1841, the Jesuits asked the sisters of the Sacred Heart to help them in their work with the Potawatomi Indians in eastern Kansas, though at 71, she couldn't master the Potawatomi language and spent much of her time in prayer. After a year, it was clear that Sister Rose's health was suffering from the rigors of life in what was still the American frontier, and she returned to the Sacred Heart convent in St. Charles, Missouri, where she lived out her remaining years in a tiny room under the stairs. She died in 1852 at the age of 83. She was canonized by Pope John Paul II in 1988.

> "Prayer reveals to souls the vanity of earthly goods and pleasures. It fills them with light, strength and consolation; and gives them a foretaste of the calm bliss of our heavenly home."
> **– St. Rose of Viterbo**

St. Rose of Viterbo had supernatural and mystical experiences from as young as age three, when she reportedly restored her deceased aunt to life. Even as a young child she was known for aiding the poor and living a life of seclusion and penance in a cell within her family's home. She is said to have been cured of a serious illness by the Blessed Virgin, who told her to join the Third Order of St. Francis and to preach penance to the people of Viterbo. At the time, Viterbo, Italy was under the rule of Emperor Frederick II of Germany but also claimed by the Vatican. Rose's street mission as a secular Franciscan was so successful that authorities exiled Rose and her family lest she stir up more supporters for the pope. From the family's refuge in Sorriano, Italy, Rose allegedly foretold the death of the emperor, which occurred eight days later. She also traveled to Vitorchiano, where the residents were said to be under the spell of a famous sorceress. Legend has it that she stood in a burning pyre for three hours and emerged unscathed, securing the conversion of the residents and the sorceress. When the pope prevailed against the emperor for control of Viterbo in 1251, Rose and her family returned. She was denied entry to the order of St. Mary of the Roses for lack of the required dowry and spent the few remaining months of her life praying and doing penance at home. She died in 1251 at the age of approximately 19 and was canonized in 1457. A 2010 examination of St. Rose of Viterbo's remains determined that she died from a rare genetic condition that even today is invariably fatal without surgical interventions.

> Apart from the cross there is no other ladder by which we may get to heaven.
> **– St. Rose of Lima**

St. Rose of Lima was born in Lima, Peru in 1586, the daughter of Spanish colonists. Her birth name was Isabel Flores de Olivia, but she was given the nickname "Rose" for her exceptional beauty, and she took Rose as her name at her confirmation. Rose always wanted to enter a convent, and as a child she lived as if she were a nun, praying, fasting, and performing penances—all in secret. As she grew into womanhood, she did her best to deter potential suitors by cutting off her hair and rubbing her face with pepper until it blistered. Her parents eventually gave up their goal of seeing her married and allowed her to cloister herself in her room, where she spent long hours in prayer, sleeping only two hours a night. She fasted daily and permanently removed all meat from her diet. She left her room only to go to Mass or to the market to sell her embroidery or flowers she raised to bring in money to help her parents and care for the poor. She often brought home the poor and the sick and took care of them in her own room. Her parents held out hope that she would marry one day, but that was not to be.

"Without the burden of afflictions it is impossible to reach the height of grace. The gift of grace increases as the struggle increases."
– **St. Rose of Lima**

Rose's parents reluctantly allowed her to join the Third Order of St. Dominic when she was 20. She took a vow of perpetual virginity and continued to live a life of great asceticism in her room in her parents' home in Lima, Peru. She imposed severe penances on herself, such as burning her hands and wearing a crown with spikes that dug into her flesh. During the eleven years of living this way, Rose gained the respect of all who knew of her piety and her efforts on behalf of the poor. When she died in 1617 at the age of 31, her funeral was attended by all the officials of Lima. It is said that she accurately predicted the date of her own death. St. Rose of Lima was beatified 50 years after her death and canonized four years later, becoming the first saint born in the Americas.

S

> "I asked you and you would not listen, so I asked my God and He did listen."
> – **St. Scholastica** (to her brother, St. Benedict of Nursia)

Sister Scholastica (c. 480 – 543) was in the habit of visiting her brother Benedict annually at a guest house near his abbey. They would spend the day praying together and discussing spiritual matters, and then Benedict would return to his cell in accordance with his Rule. The legend maintains that during their last visit, Scholastic had a premonition that she would soon die and asked her brother to stay longer. When he said that he couldn't, Scholastic folded her hands and prayed silently, and moments later a violent storm began to rage around the guest house. Benedict asked her "What have you done?" and she replied, "I asked you and you would not listen, so I asked my God and He did listen." Because of the storm, Benedict could not return to his cell, and brother and sister spent the entire night in discussion. Three days later Scholastica died, and at the moment of her death, Benedict reportedly saw her soul ascending to heaven in the form of a white dove.

> "The devil strains every nerve to secure the souls which belong to Christ. We should not grudge our toil in wresting them from Satan and giving them back to God."
> – **St. Sebastian**

Much of what is known about the martyrdom of St. Sebastian comes from a sermon written by St. Ambrose of Milan. According to tradition, Sebastian, a Christian, joined the Roman army in the year 283 to do whatever he could to help those who were being martyred during Emperor Diocletian's persecution of Christians. He is credited with converting several Romans, including the local prefect, who released all his prisoners from jail. Several of Sebastian's converts were later martyred. In 286, Sebastian's identity as a Christian was discovered, and the emperor ordered him to be bound to a stake in a field to be shot full of arrows by archers. Left for dead, he was nursed back to health by Irene of Rome, the widow of the martyred St. Castulus. Two years later, Sebastian was condemned a second time when he stood in a spot the emperor would soon pass and berated him for his persecution of Christians. Diocletian ordered him beaten to death with cudgels and had his body thrown into the sewer. A pious Christian woman removed the body and buried it in the catacombs.

> "You desire that which exceeds my humble powers, but I trust in the compassion and mercy of the all-powerful God."
> – **St. Stephen**

St. Stephen (5 AD – 34 AD) was the eldest of the first seven men to be ordained as deacons of the Church and was named archdeacon. He was also the first Christian martyr. He is believed to have been Jewish, and he was tried by the Sanhedrin for blasphemy against God and Moses. During his trial, Stephen spoke eloquently and quoted from Hebrew Scriptures. He also chastised the Sanhedrin for persecuting the prophets who foretold the birth of the Messiah and for the betrayal and death of Jesus. At the end of his testimony, Stephen saw a vision of Jesus standing at the right hand of God, and he told the Sanhedrin what he saw. His words enraged the crowd, who rushed in, seized him, and carried him away to stone him to death. St. Stephen's last words as stones rained down upon him echoed the words of Jesus on the Cross, forgiving the very people who were killing him.

> "There is more value in a little study of humility and in a single act of it than in all the knowledge in the world."
> – **St. Teresa of Avila**

St. Teresa of Avila's name at her birth in Avila, Spain in 1515 was Teresa Ali Fatim Corella Sanchez de Capeda y Ahumada. Her father was a wealthy man, the son of a converted Jew who had been condemned by the Inquisition for returning to Judaism. Her parents' marriage was not a happy one. Teresa often found herself caught in the middle between her sternly pious father and her mother, who hid the romance novels she loved and begged her daughter not to give away her secret. Should she lie to her father, who insisted on honesty in all matters, or betray her mother? She realized in her childhood that she did not want that kind of marriage for herself. The death of her mother when Teresa was only 11 devastated her and left her father all the more determined that his daughter behave properly.

"From silly devotions and sour-faced saints, good Lord, deliver us!"
– **St. Teresa of Avila**

Teresa was a somewhat rebellious teenager, preoccupied with thoughts of boys and stylish clothes, but her strict father's reaction to her behavior had her convinced that she was very sinful. Believing her to be out of control, he sent her to a Carmelite convent at 16. At first, she viewed it as punishment, but in time she came to like convent life. When she had to decide whether to remain in the convent and take vows or return to the secular world and marry, she was swayed by her fear of ending up like her mother, under the thumb of a stern and demanding husband.

> "The more we see that any action springs not from the motive of obedience, the more evident is it that it is a temptation of the enemy; for when God sends an inspiration, the very first effect of it is to infuse a spirit of docility."
> **– St. Teresa of Avila**

Though Teresa didn't think being a nun would be fun, she thought a convent was probably the best place for someone as sinful as she believed herself to be. But life as a nun was not as Teresa had envisioned it. In Teresa's time, many women entered a convent for lack of anywhere else to go or anything else to do with their lives. Nuns often tried to make themselves attractive and entertained male visitors in the parlor. Money mattered. It conferred status and popularity in a way that piety did not. Teresa was easily distracted from her attempts to practice mental prayer by worldly thoughts and desires. She wanted to be liked, which meant acting the way the sisters she wanted to be friends with acted. She found it hard to keep Jesus in her mind, even when teaching mental prayer to visitors to bring in their donations to help the community financially. As much as Teresa wanted to immerse herself in prayer, she found it very difficult.

> "Our body has this defect that, the more it is provided care and comforts, the more needs and desires it finds."
> – **St. Teresa of Avila**

For many years in the convent, Teresa strived to learn how to practice mental prayer, which was based on principles favored by medieval mystics, such as the examination of one's conscience, spiritual self-concentration, and inner contemplation. A serious bout of malaria left Teresa paralyzed for three years and permanently compromised her health. Her condition gave her plenty of excuses not to pray. When those excuses grew old, she blamed her failure to pray often or well on her sinful nature, because sinners didn't deserve to ask anything of God. At the urging of a priest, she went back to praying when she was 41 but found it almost impossible to quiet her thoughts and focus on God. As she grew more diligent about praying in her forties, Teresa began to have mystical experiences including raptures and even levitation. She viewed these as God's way of chastising her and getting her to change her behavior.

"We always find that those who walked closest to Christ were those who had to bear the greatest trials."
– **St. Teresa of Avila**

Once Teresa began praying in earnest, she began having more and more mystical experiences. She found it uncomfortable to have her ecstasies witnessed by others and begged God not to give her any more "favors" in public. Still, her strong attachment to her friends sometimes distracted her during prayer until God told her that henceforth she should speak only with angels, not human beings. Teresa said that after hearing those words, she was finally able to put God first in her prayers and in her life.

"We are preparing ourselves for the time, which will come very soon, when we shall find ourselves at the end of our journey and shall be drinking of living water from the fountain I have described. Unless we make a total surrender of our will to the Lord and put ourselves in His hands so that He may do in all things what is best for us in accordance with His will, He will never allow us to drink of it."
– **St. Teresa of Avila**

After God told Teresa in a vision to speak only with angels, not humans, her friends were unhappy about being cut off from her. They asked a Jesuit to determine whether she had been tricked by the devil into giving up human companionship. His conclusion that Teresa's visions were indeed of divine origin subjected her to ridicule by many. However, a confessor agreed with Teresa's friends that her visions were from the devil and told her to make an obscene gesture whenever she thought she saw Jesus. She complied, but apologized to Jesus, who told her she was doing the right thing by obeying her confessor's instructions. She eventually concluded that the peace, inspiration, and encouragement she got from her visions were proof that they were from God.

> "Now and then, I am amazed at the evil one bad companion can do—nor could I believe it if I did not know it by experience—especially when we are young: then is it that the evil must be greatest. Oh, that parents would take warning by me, and look carefully to this!"
> – **St. Teresa of Avila**

Teresa eventually decided that if she wanted an environment that was more conducive to the kind of religious life she sought, then she would found a new, reformed Carmelite convent dedicated to a simple, contemplative life of poverty and prayer. Her decision was met with criticism from all sides. Even when threatened with the Inquisition and legal action by the town, Teresa remained calm and determined, and was supported in her decision by the bishop and by her spiritual guide and counselor, the Franciscan priest, St. Peter of Alcantara. She founded the convent of St. Joseph in Avila in 1562 and received papal approval for her Rule of strict poverty, which she set forth in a "constitution" and a set of regulations that included weekly ceremonial flagellation and discalceation (the practice of going barefoot). The next five years were, for Teresa, a period of seclusion and writing her Life, as she had been ordered to do to clear herself with the Inquisition.

> "There is no such thing as bad weather. All weather is good because it is God's."
> **– St. Teresa of Avila**

Teresa ran the convent she founded, St. Joseph's, with a spirit of love. Yes, her guiding principles were strict, but they were intended to bring the sisters closer to God by changing their behavior to please Him, not through acts of penance. She believed in working at increasing one's obedience to God, and she also regarded poverty as an incentive to work to support the convent without begging. She encouraged the sisters to walk about in nature when their spirits needed lifting because it would help them appreciate the wonders of God's creation.

"A truly humble person never believes that he can be wronged in anything. Truly, we ought to be shamed to resent whatever is said or done against us; for it is the greatest shame in the world to see that our Creator bears so many insults from His creatures, and that we resent even a little word that is contradictory."
– **St. Teresa of Avila**

At the age of 51, Teresa was granted a patent from the Carmelite general to establish new convents to spread her reform movement. For the next four years she traveled all over Spain, braving some very difficult conditions, and founded seven more convents. In addition to the rigors of travel and negotiating with property owners and financial supporters, Teresa had to cope with downright hostility from several directions. When the nuns in her former Carmelite convent elected her prioress, they were excommunicated by the leader of the Carmelite order, and a law officer was posted outside the convent door to prevent her from entering. Other religious orders in the towns where she wanted to open new convents opposed her to the point that she feared causing a riot wherever she went. The papal nuncio called her a "restless, disobedient gadabout." She was denounced to the Inquisition by a princess who ordered Teresa to found a convent and then became enraged by Teresa's refusal to order the nuns to wait on the princess on their knees. Such incidents only strengthened Teresa's resolve.

> "Those who can enclose within the little paradise of the soul Him who created heaven and earth, may well believe they are in a good road, and that they shall not fail to arrive at length at the fountain of life, because they will make great progress in a short time."
> – **St. Teresa of Avila**

After founding convents for women all over Spain, Teresa secured the help of John of the Cross and Anthony of Jesus to establish houses for men. The first convent of Discalced Carmelite Brethren was established in 1568. It was followed by four more houses for men between 1571 and 1576. The growing popularity of Teresa's reforms resulted in increased opposition from the older Carmelite order. They forbade her to found any more convents, and she was forced to voluntarily retire to one of her own houses. She chose to retire to St. Joseph's, the first convent she founded, back in 1562, but inquisitions were launched against the friends who had helped her spread her reforms. It took several years of letter-writing to get King Philip II to have the inquisitions halted in 1579 and establish protections for continued reform efforts. Teresa was finally able to emerge from her forced retirement and continue her life's work.

"There are more tears shed over answered prayers than over unanswered prayers."
– **St. Teresa of Avila**

Teresa spent 20 years of her life traveling throughout Spain spreading her reforms and establishing convents for Discalced Carmelite nuns and men's cloisters. In 1582, she fell ill on one of her journeys and died at the age of 67. Her last words were "My Lord, it is time to move on. Well then, may your will be done. O my Lord and my Spouse, the hour that I have longed for has come. It is time to meet one another." Only 40 years after her death she was canonized by Pope Gregory XV and was named Doctor of the Church by Pope Paul VI in 1970, at the same time as St. Catherine of Siena, making them the first two women to be awarded that honor.

> "Truth suffers, but never dies."
> – **St. Teresa of Avila**

In 1970, St. Teresa of Avila was named a Doctor of the Church, the Doctor of Prayer—a fitting honor for one who struggled so mightily to learn how to pray. The autobiography she penned during her five years of seclusion after founding her first convent described how the soul ascends toward union with God in four stages: 1) Devotion of Heart, 2) Devotion of Peace, 3) Devotion of Union, and 4) Devotion of Ecstasy. Her description of each stage is based on her own personal experiences and spiritual growth. Devotion to the Heart captures the struggles of the soul to focus inwardly through mental prayer. Devotion of Peace is the surrender of human will to God, though the soul is not yet immune to distraction. Devotion of Union is a mystical and ecstatic state in which the soul is absorbed in God, conferring a blissful peace. In the final stage, Devotion of Ecstasy, the soul is no longer conscious of the body, and the body, in a trance-like state may levitate off the ground, as Teresa is reported to have done on several occasions during Mass.

> "Love to be real, it must cost—it must hurt—it must empty us of self."
> **– St. Teresa of Calcutta**

During all the years that she worked with the poor, Mother Teresa struggled with a profound spiritual darkness. The more she longed to feel God's love, the harder it was for her to feel any connection to Him. She called this darkness the "painful night" of her soul, yet nobody, not even those closest to her, knew what she was experiencing. Her postulator likened it to the "dark night of the soul" described by St. John of the Cross or St. Therese of Lisieux's "night of nothing." Mother Teresa's "painful night" allowed her to share in Jesus' spiritual agony on the Cross and longing for love, even as she shared in the lonely desolation of the poor and sought a deeper relationship with God. This darkness began shortly after she received her "call within a call" through a series of mystical experiences in which Jesus revealed His sorrow over the plight of the poor and the fact that they did not know Him. After twenty years of teaching, she heeded Jesus' call to establish the Missionaries of Charity to serve the poorest of the poor.

> "I know God will not give me anything I can't handle. I just wish He didn't trust me so much."
> **– St. Teresa of Calcutta**

The first half of Mother Teresa's religious life was relatively uneventful. Albanian-born Agnes Gonxha Bojaxhiu left home at age 18 to join the Institute of the Blessed Virgin Mary, better known as the Sisters of Loreto, in Ireland and took the name Sister Mary Teresa in honor of St. Therese of Lisieux. The following year she was sent to India, and in 1931 was assigned to teach at St. Mary's School for girls, which she did happily until she was called by Jesus to found the Missionaries of Charity. She worked alone initially, walking through the poorest sections of Calcutta and rendering whatever aid she could. One after another of her former St. Mary's students joined her, and the Missionaries of Charity had its official beginning in 1950. It was followed in 1963 by the Missionaries of Charity Brothers, in 1976 and 1979 by the contemplative branch of the Sisters and the Brothers respectively, and in 1984 by the Missionaries of Charity Fathers. She also founded several organizations to allow those without religious vocations to participate in her work among the poor. By the time of her death in 1997, there were nearly 4,000 members in 610 foundations in 123 nations.

> "Joy is a net of love by which we catch souls."
> – **St. Teresa of Calcutta**

For many people living today, St. Teresa of Calcutta is a familiar figure. We saw photos of the diminutive nun in her white, blue-bordered sari accepting the Nobel Prize for Peace in 1979 "for the glory of God and in the name of the poor." Again and again, we saw Mother Teresa of Calcutta's name on lists of the most admired people, including in the top spot in the 1999 Gallup's List of the Most Widely Admired People of the 20th Century, ahead of Martin Luther King, Jr. and John F. Kennedy. Her 2016 canonization by Pope Francis was televised live and streamed online. Yet she was not without her critics. Many claimed that her service to the poor wasn't aimed at helping them as much as it was intended to make converts for the Church. But Mother Teresa's mission was not to eliminate poverty in India, or in any of the other places in the world where the Missionaries of Charity, the order she founded, had a presence. Rather, it was to serve God among "the unwanted, the unloved, the uncared for" and to help them know God's love. And that is exactly what she did.

> "For me prayer is a surge of the heart, it is a simple look towards Heaven, it is a cry of recognition and of love, embracing both trial and joy."
> **– St. Therese of Lisieux**

St. Therese of Lisieux is one of the most popular of all the saints because people find it easy to relate to her. She lived a simple life, wrote plainly, and showed that simple acts done with love enabled one to grow in holiness. She had a childlike quality, an innocence and purity of heart, which was not surprising given the fact that she entered religious life as a child of fifteen and would have done so even earlier if she had been permitted to. Though she'd been raised in a devout family, had older sisters who had already entered convents, and had been practicing mental prayer since she was eleven without ever having been taught how, Therese said that Jesus truly came into her heart when she was fourteen on Christmas day. As the youngest of five sisters, motherless from the age of four, she was the pampered "baby," and prone to tantrums. But on that day, an incident that would have normally triggered a tantrum suffused her with love.

> "You cannot be half a saint; you must be a whole saint or no saint at all."
> – **St. Therese of Lisieux**

When Therese was ten, she contracted an illness that caused her temperature to soar. She was so ill that her survival was in question. She hated having people sitting at her bedside staring at her like, as she put it, "a string of onion." Her sisters were praying to a statue of the Blessed Virgin in her room, and she began to pray along with them. When she saw Mary smile at her, she was cured instantly. Those who witnessed the event told others, and soon Therese was being bombarded with questions that struck her as trivial. What was she wearing? What did she look like? She refused to answer them, and her interrogators spread the rumor that she lied about seeing Mary just to get attention.

> "One must have passed through the tunnel to understand how black its darkness is."
> – **St. Therese of Lisieux**

By the time Therese was an adolescent, three of her sisters had entered convents, leaving only her sister Celine at home with her and their father. Pauline was a Carmelite, as was Marie, and Leonie joined the Poor Clares. Therese wanted to join Pauline and Marie in the Carmelite convent, but the superior refused her entry because of her age. So did the bishop, but Therese was nothing if not determined and persistent. Her father and Celine took her to Rome, thinking it would distract her, but Therese had another plan. The family was given an audience with the pope, but they were all instructed not to speak to him. Therese, however, shouted out to the pope, begging him to allow her to enter the Carmelite convent and was physically carried out by two guards. Fortunately for Therese, the Vicar General had witnessed the incident and so admired her bravery that he approved her admission to the convent.

> "What beauty? I don't see my beauty at all; I see only the graces I've received from God. You always misunderstand me; you don't know, then, that I'm only a little seedling, a little almond."
> **– St. Therese of Lisieux**

Therese's adjustment to life as a cloistered nun was a difficult one. Not long after she entered the convent, her father suffered the first of several strokes that resulted in both physical and mental impairment, and he was confined to an insane asylum. She was distraught at not being able to leave the convent to visit him. In her grief, she found it hard to pray. She not only felt powerless to help her father, but also unable to do anything great enough to show God the depth of her love for Him. Small of stature and unable to do great deeds, she concluded that if she did enough small deeds and made enough small sacrifices, she could prove her love. She wrote, "Great deeds are forbidden me. The only way I can prove my love is by scattering flowers and these flowers are every little sacrifice, every glance and word, and the doing of the least actions for love."

"Let us go forward in peace, our eyes upon heaven, the only one goal of our labors."
– **St. Therese of Lisieux**

Therese showed her love for God through obedience, sacrifice, and by showing love for everyone around her. She did things she didn't want to do, ate things she didn't want to eat, was nice to sisters she didn't like, begged forgiveness for things she didn't do, and ultimately agreed, when her sister Pauline was elected prioress, to remain a perpetual novice. Therese not only aspired to be holy, but to become a saint: "God would not make me wish for something impossible and so, in spite of my littleness, I can aim at being a saint." The way for her to get to heaven, she concluded, was by making love her vocation."

> True love is found only in complete self-forgetfulness, and it is only after we have detached ourselves from every creature that we find Jesus.
> – **St. Therese of Lisieux**

At the age of 23, Therese realized she had the unmistakable symptoms of tuberculosis, but she kept her illness a secret for a year before it became apparent to everyone in the convent. She suffered not only immense physical pain but also the pain of thinking she would die without having accomplished anything and that nobody would remember her. But she had been keeping a journal, and her sister Pauline, who was like a second mother to her, encouraged her to keep writing. After Therese died at age 24, Pauline circulated her writings to other convents, and her "little way" of making small daily sacrifices resonated with ordinary Catholics who wanted to find holiness. In her short time on earth, "little" Therese made a big impact, and she has continued to do so ever since. She was canonized as St. Therese of Lisieux (the town she grew up in) in 1925.

> "Obedience unites us so closely to God that in a way transforms us into Him, so that we have no other will but His. If obedience is lacking, even prayer cannot be pleasing to God."
> **– St. Thomas Aquinas**

The custom among well-to-do families in 13th century Italy was for the youngest son to enter a monastery. Thomas's parents, of minor nobility, entrusted his education to the Benedictines and assumed he would join the Benedictine order in time. But when Thomas had completed his early education, he informed his parents that he had decided to join the recently founded Dominican order, a decision made largely due to the influence of a Dominican preacher he met at the university in Naples. In fact, he had already secretly become a Dominican in 1244. His parents were so opposed to the idea that they had his brothers kidnap him and bring him home, where he was held captive for a year while they tried to change his mind. His family did everything they could think of to separate Thomas from the Dominicans, including hiring a prostitute to seduce him. As the story goes, Thomas fended her off with a fireplace iron. His mother eventually realized they were waging a losing battle and decided to live with her son's decision, though she didn't want to let the rest of the family know she had given in. In 1244, she allowed him to "escape."

> In the life of the body, a man is sometimes sick, and unless he takes medicine, he will die. Even so in the spiritual life a man is sick on account of sin. For that reason he needs medicine so that he may be restored to health; and this grace is bestowed in the Sacrament of Penance.
> **– St. Thomas Aquinas**

From 1245 to 1272, Thomas completed his education, was ordained as a Dominican priest, became a master teacher, and wrote prolifically on Catholic theology—both scholarly texts for advanced students and his most famous but unfinished work, *Summa Theologica*, aimed at beginning students. His studies, teaching, and preaching took him to Naples, Paris, and Cologne. He was in great demand by both universities and religious institutions. At the request of the Dominicans, he established a university in Naples and served as regent master. Not long after, for some unexplained reason, Thomas stopped writing and teaching, saying only that "All that I have written seems like straw to me." He died less than three months later, in March 1274.

> "The Blessed Eucharist is the perfect Sacrament of the Lord's Passion, since It contains Christ Himself and his Passion."
> **– St. Thomas Aquinas**

St. Thomas Aquinas had, and continues to have, a tremendous influence on ecclesiastical architecture. In his writings on beauty, he identified three qualities that all beautiful things have in common: integritas, consonantia, and claritas. Integritas refers to wholeness—having everything that is essential and nothing that isn't. Consonantia has to do with proportionality; the dimensions of a beautiful thing are appropriate to its purpose and the "goal that God had in mind for it." Claritas is radiance, or the light that radiates from a thing of beauty and illuminates purpose and meaning. This aesthetic underlies the design of churches today just as it did in the 13th century.

> "To one who has faith, no explanation is necessary. To one without faith, no explanation is possible."
> – **St. Thomas Aquinas**

There are few medieval writers whose philosophical works are still read, studied, and debated today, and St. Thomas Aquinas is one of them. During his 48 years on earth, he wrote 60 works of various lengths. His prodigious output was due in part to having an incredible memory for everything he had ever read and studied. St. Antoninus described Thomas's mind as being like a huge library. He was also given the great grace of, in his own words, "understanding whatever I have read." Thomas was also a master of multi-tasking, often dictating several works to as many as five scribes at a time.

> "Charity is the form, mover, mother and root of all the virtues."
> **– St. Thomas Aquinas**

St. Thomas Aquinas described charity as a form of friendship, but without the caveats imposed by Aristotle and other philosophers, such as the notion that friendship can only exist between beings who are equal in dignity. According to Thomas, charity is above all a friendship with God. God shares his own friendship, his love, with us, though we are far below Him in dignity. We in turn share it with others, even our enemies, for the sake of God. It does not require us to have anything in common with those we are charitable toward other than the love God has for all his creation. The love that God calls upon us to have for sinners is the essence of charity.

> "Faith has to do with things that are not seen, and hope with things that are not in hand."
> – **St. Thomas Aquinas**

Unlike many of his contemporaries among ecclesiastical scholars and philosophers, St. Thomas Aquinas did not view faith and reason as mutually exclusive but rather as divine gifts from God the Creator. He never studied without first praying for insight and understanding, and when insight and understanding were slow in coming, he would also fast. He had tremendous influence on theologians and philosophers alike. St. Francis de Sales, St. Philip Neri, St. Charles Borromeo, St. Vincent Ferrer, Pope St. Pius V, and St. Antoninus are all known to have been avid students of the works of St. Thomas Aquinas. Among philosophers, he has been referred to as the "Christian Aristotle." In his encyclical, *Aeterni Patris*, Pope Leo XIII said that "reason, borne on the wings of Thomas, can scarcely rise higher, while faith could scarcely expect more or stronger aids from reason than those which she has already obtained through Thomas."

> "Shun useless conversation. We lose by it both time and the spirit of devotion."
> **– St. Thomas Aquinas**

Those who knew St. Thomas Aquinas attested to the divine assistance he received in the form of visions and ecstasies. Thomas himself said that he learned more through prayer and contemplation than from studying the words of men. His contemporaries wrote of the Blessed Virgin appearing to him to let him know that both his life and his work found favor with God. St. Peter and St. Paul reportedly helped him interpret a difficult Scripture passage, and St. Dominic encouraged him to overcome his concerns about being unworthy to receive a doctorate.

"Fear is such a powerful emotion for humans that when we allow it to take us over, it drives compassion right out of our hearts."
– **St. Thomas Aquinas**

St. Thomas Aquinas described two types of fear: servile fear and filial fear. Servile fear helps keep us from sinning because we fear God's punishment. Filial fear, however, keeps us from sinning because we fear offending and being separated from the Father. It is filial fear that is counted among the seven gifts of the Holy Ghost. According to Thomas, "filial fear and hope cling together and perfect one another." So, while fear itself is not a theological virtue, in the view of Thomas Aquinas, it works with theological virtues like hope, love, and faith towards our salvation.

> "Tribulation is a gift from God—one that he especially gives His special friends."
> – **St. Thomas More**

Thomas More endured great tribulations toward the end of his life, all in service of God and the Catholic Church. Most people remember him for his defense of the Church against King Henry VIII's declaration that the king was not subject to papal rule, which led to the establishment of the Church of England. Though Thomas More would be martyred and eventually canonized for his refusal to acknowledge King Henry VIII as head of the Church in England, he was not a cleric himself, but rather a lawyer. There was a point in his life when Thomas did contemplate giving up the practice of law in favor of religious life. For two years (1503-1504), he lived next door to a Carthusian monastery. He was so impressed by their simple life of piety that he joined in their spiritual exercises, but he ultimately chose to remain in the secular world.

> "Either Christ has a Church in the world continually and until the end of the world, or else He has a Church sometimes, and sometimes not at all. Could we think that He had a Church while He was here Himself, and perhaps awhile after, but mysteriously none since? . . . No . . . that can in no way be, since He must necessarily still preserve His Church somewhere; otherwise, how could He be with His followers continually until the end of the world?"
> – **St. Thomas More**

Thomas More was first elected to Parliament in 1504, married, and rose through the ranks to the position of Privy Counselor in 1514. When he married Jane Colt in 1505, it was for love. They had four children together before Jane died in 1512. His second marriage, less than a month after Jane's death, seems to have been motivated by a need to provide a stepmother to care for his four motherless children. Alice Harpur Middleton, a wealthy widow with one child fit the bill, though she was neither attractive nor particularly agreeable. Those who knew Thomas disapproved of his choice for a second wife and with the haste of the marriage. By all reports, it was not a happy marriage, but Thomas adopted Alice's daughter and treated her as one of his own children. It is certainly fitting that St. Thomas More is the patron saint of difficult marriages and adopted children (as well as lawyers, politicians, and civil servants).

> "The Devil never runs upon a man to seize him with his claws until he sees him on the ground, already having fallen by his own will."
> **– St. Thomas More**

King Henry VIII recognized Thomas More's legal acumen and his standing as a theologian and writer and rewarded him with positions of increasing responsibility and trust. In turn, the king had Thomas More's complete loyalty. In 1529, More was made Lord Chancellor, and for nine years, he staunchly defended the Catholic faith in England, prosecuting heretics and justifying Henry's confidence in him. The turning point came in 1530 while Henry was attempting to get his marriage to his wife Catherine annulled so that he could marry Anne Boleyn. He asked Thomas to sign a letter to the pope supporting the king's annulment request. Thomas refused. The relationship between the king and his Lord Chancellor deteriorated with each step Henry took to defy papal authority. In 1532, Thomas More resigned rather than continue in a position that was antithetical to his identity and values as a Catholic. The following year, he chose to write a letter of congratulations rather than attend Anne Boleyn's coronation as Queen of England. Henry saw that as an affront and an offense and started building a case against him. Thomas used his considerable legal skills to counter the bogus charges, but the breaking point came in 1534 when More voiced all but one of the attestations included in an oath he was required to take. He agreed to accept Anne as queen and the legitimacy of the marriage, but he refused to acknowledge the king as the head of the church. That refusal sealed his fate.

> "A faint faith is better than a strong heresy."
> – **St. Thomas More**

When Thomas More went on trial for treason in 1534, he faced a jury that included three of Anne Boleyn's relatives: her brother, father, and uncle. It was his refusal to endorse King Henry XIII's request for an annulment of his marriage to Queen Catherine in order to marry Anne that triggered the events that led Thomas to this point. It took the court only fifteen minutes to convict him and impose the usual sentence for treason 16th century England: hanging, drawing, and quartering. Henry showed a measure of mercy for his former Lord Chancellor by commuting the sentence to decapitation. Standing on the scaffold for his refusal to acknowledge King Henry VIII as head of the Church in England, his final words to observers were "the king's good servant, but God's first." Pope Leo XIII beatified More as a martyr in 1886, and Pope Pius XI canonized him in 1935.

"If you want God to hear your prayers, hear the voice of the poor. If you wish God to anticipate your wants, provide those of the needy without waiting for them to ask you. Especially anticipate the needs of those who are ashamed to beg. To make them ask for alms is to make them buy it."
– **St. Thomas of Villanova**

Though he was Archbishop of Valencia, Spain, Thomas of Villanova cut a rather shabby and somewhat comical figure, the typical absent-minded, shabbily dressed, professor. He was referred to during his life as "the almsgiver" and "the father of the poor" for his great charity toward the poor and unfortunate, with a special affinity for orphans, the sick, and poor women lacking dowries. He lived with great austerity, frequently giving away his own possessions to those who were in need. He wore the same habit for decades, mending it himself until it practically fell apart. He sold the straw mattress he slept on and gave the money to the poor. When he was given funds by his cathedral chapter to furnish and decorate his residence, Archbishop Thomas donated the money to repair a local hospital. Nobody that came to the door of the residence was turned away without being fed and given some money. While he was personally generous to a fault, Thomas's approach to charity was a practical one aimed not only at meeting the immediate needs of the poor but also helping them learn to help themselves. On his deathbed, Thomas of Villanova gave instructions for the distribution of all his money to the poor.

"He who is humble easily obeys everyone, fears to offend anyone, is at peace with everyone, is kind with all."
– **St. Thomas of Villanova**

When Thomas of Villanova reluctantly became Archbishop of Valencia in 1544, he was taking on the governance of an Archdiocese in which the top position had remained vacant for a century. He approached his mission in a very practical and methodical manner. He conducted his own assessment by visiting every parish to see firsthand what needs existed—social as well as religious. He established a college for Moorish converts, founded a seminary, and implemented a plan to provide social services and charitable assistance for the Moors and others in need. Everything he did was intended to return the archdiocese to health—spiritually and materially. The list of his efforts and accomplishments includes: addressing social ills such as violence, divorce, concubinage; closing the underground prisons; establishing an orphanage; holding Mass early enough for working class people to attend; and holding laypeople and clergy alike to a higher moral standard.

"Dismiss all anger and look a little into yourself. Remember that he of whom you are speaking is your brother, and, as he is in the way of salvation, God can make him a Saint, notwithstanding his present weaknesses. You may fall into the same faults or perhaps into a worse fault. But supposing that you remain upright, to whom are you indebted for it, if not to the pure mercy of God?"
– **St. Thomas of Villanova**

St. Thomas got his surname from Vilanova de los Infantes, the town where he was educated, not from the town of his birth in 1488, Fuenlana in Castile. He got his charitable disposition from his parents, who were known for their help to the poor, though they were of modest means themselves. They sold only as much of their corn crop as was necessary to meet he family's basic needs, using the rest of it to bake bread to distribute to the poor. In fact, a good portion of everything that was produced on their small estate was earmarked for the needy. As a little boy, Thomas was displaying the same charitable nature. When he had no way to meet a need on his own, he would ask his parents to help him provide. Even in childhood, Thomas saw a personally austere life as the way to give more to the poor.

> "You must never ask Jesus to wait."
> – **St. Ursula Ledochowska**

Julia Maria Ledochowska, born in Austria in 1865, needed to look no farther than her own family for examples of piety and holiness. Her uncle was Primate of Poland, and her older sister founded the Missionary Sisters of St. Peter Claver. The family moved to Poland when Julia Maria was eighteen, and she entered the convent of the Ursuline Sisters in Krakow, taking the name "Maria Ursula of Jesus" and dedicating her life to children. In 1907, Mother Ursula, now the convent's prioress, went with another nun to St. Petersburg, Russia at the request of Monsignor Constantine Budkiewicz, where they founded a new convent and worked with immigrant children. When World War I broke out seven years later, Mother Ursula, still an Austrian citizen, was expelled and fled to Sweden, and the Monsignor, a Polish national, was martyred by the Bolsheviks. In neutral Sweden, Mother Ursula worked tirelessly on behalf of Poles living in exile, and when Poland regained its independence in 1918, she and her Ursuline sisters returned to Poland with dozens of orphans. She founded her own Congregation, the Ursuline Sisters of the Heart of Jesus in Agony, dedicated to educating and training children and youth and serving the poor and oppressed. The congregation expanded, with new houses and missions in Poland, Italy, and France. She continued her work until her death in 1939, as Europe was once again on the brink of war.

V

> "Charity is certainly greater than any rule. Moreover, all rules must lead to charity."
> – **St. Vincent de Paul**

St. Vincent de Paul, born in 1581, earned the money to finance his studies in theology at the University of Toulouse by tutoring the children of a wealthy family. Five years after his ordination, the ship Vincent was traveling on was captured, and he was sold as a slave in Tunis. He escaped and returned to France two years later. Most of his life was devoted to preaching missions and helping the poor, and later, convicts as well. The need was greater than he could meet on his own, so he established the Ladies of Charity, a lay institute for women, and a religious institute called the Congregation of Priests of the Missions, commonly known today as the Vincentians. One of his goals was to improve the instruction and development of priests, and his work toward that end laid the foundation for today's seminaries.

"We should strive to keep our hearts open to the sufferings and wretchedness of other people and pray continually that God may grant us that spirit of compassion which is truly the spirit of God."
– **St. Vincent de Paul**

The events in the life of St. Vincent de Paul that took place after the ship he was traveling on was captured by Barbary pirates read like an adventure novel. He was sold as a slave and underwent several changes in ownership before he escaped. He was sold first to a fisherman but was resold quickly because he got too seasick to work on a boat. His second owner was a spagyrical physician—part herbalist and part alchemist—whose work Vincent found very interesting. When the physician died, Vincent was sold to a French former priest and Franciscan who had converted to Islam and had three wives. One of his wives, a Muslim, had conversations with Vincent about his faith and came to believe that Christianity is the true faith, a conclusion the shared with her husband. He admitted that he regretted renouncing Christianity, and he resolved to flee back to France and take his slave, Vincent, with him. They made their escape some months later in a small boat, landing on French soil in June 1607.

"It is God Himself who receives what we give in charity, and is it not an incomparable happiness to give Him what belongs to Him, and what we have received from His goodness alone?"
– **St. Vincent de Paul**

In 1617, Father Vincent became parish priest of Chatillon·les-Dombes, France. His first sermon there so inspired two society matrons that they gave up worldly diversions in favor of doing good in their community. One of them brought to Father Vincent's attention a family stricken with illness that was making it difficult for them to tend one another's needs. Father Vincent's sermon in charity that Sunday resulted in the afflicted family being inundated with food, leading him to conclude that charitable efforts need to be better coordinated. He met with the women, and they agreed to establish an association of women who would take turns providing for the poor. This Confraternity of Charity, also known as the Ladies of Charity, was for lay women, and it was an essential element of Father Vincent's approach to renewing the Church in the countryside: a mission followed by the establishment of a Confraternity of Charity to continue building the Christian community.

"You must ask God to give you power to fight against the sin of pride which is your greatest enemy – the root of all that is evil, and the failure of all that is good. For God resists the proud."
– **St. Vincent de Paul**

The Confraternities of Charity, or simply "Charities," were established by Father Vincent as part of his strategy for conducting missions as he traveled throughout the French countryside. Wherever there was a mission, a new Charity would be founded to carry on the work of the mission. Different village charities had somewhat different rules, but in general, there were to be 20 members of each Charity—each a virtuous woman, married or single, whose family agreed with her decision to become a "servant of the poor." Meeting one Sunday a month, taking turns visiting and caring for the sick and poor, being devout Catholics, and serving Jesus Christ in the person of the poor—that was the commitment they made. In some villages, male Charities called Priests and Brothers of the Mission were established as well to assist the indigent and to provide job training for youth.

"If humble souls are contradicted, they remain calm; if they are calumniated, they suffer with patience; if they are little esteemed, neglected, or forgotten, they consider that their due; if they are weighed down with occupations, they perform them cheerfully."
– **St. Vincent de Paul**

By 1629, it became apparent to Father Vincent that the Charities he and the priests assisting him had been establishing with each mission were too numerous for him to oversee. He enlisted Louise de Marillac to follow right on the heels of the Missionists, setting up new Charities, visiting existing ones, providing encouragement, and getting things organized. She took on the task with enthusiasm, modeling servitude to the poor while organizing, recruiting and training new members, caring for the sick, and educating poor children. In some wealthier parishes in Paris, the society ladies volunteering to become servants of the poor lacked practical skills and were unaccustomed to doing any real work. Thus was born the Daughters of Charity in 1633, to help the ladies in doing the work of their Charities.

> "The most powerful weapon to conquer the devil is humility. For, as he does not know at all how to employ it, neither does he know how to defend himself from it."
> **– St. Vincent de Paul**

In founding the Daughters of Charity, St. Vincent de Paul and St. Louise de Marillac envisioned a group of religious women who would move freely and serve in the community, but at the time, the French government wanted nuns to be cloistered. Not wanting to draw attention to the Daughters of Charity, they didn't use the term "sister" in referring to the women. The Daughters of Charity were unlike other orders of their time, and the same distinctions exist today. For example, they make annual vows, not lifetime ones. No vows are said at all until five years after the date that a young woman enters the seminary. At that point she pronounces vows for the first time and will repeat them every subsequent year. Vincent and Louise didn't want the Daughters of Charity to be set apart in any way from the people they served, so rather than a traditional habit, the Daughters wore the clothing of a French peasant woman, complete with sunbonnet.

"Give me a person of prayer, and such a one will be capable of accomplishing anything."
– **St. Vincent de Paul**

St. Vincent de Paul is the patron saint of all charities, among them the Society of St. Vincent de Paul, founded in 1833, by Blessed Frédéric Ozanam. The Society of St, Vincent de Paul is a Catholic lay organization of men and women seeking spiritual growth through personal service to the poor and suffering. Members, known as Vincentians, come from diverse backgrounds but adhere to the same basic Rule. The Society of St. Vincent de Paul differs from other charitable organizations that aim to do good for others without concern for their members' spiritual advancement. Vincentians do good because they see the face of Christ in every person they help. In 2016, nearly 1,000 trained volunteers in the U.S. alone donated 17.5 million hours of volunteer service to nearly 21 million people in their homes, in prisons, and in hospitals.

"Humility is nothing but truth, and pride is nothing but lying."
– **St. Vincent de Paul**

St. Vincent de Paul identified five characteristic virtues of a missionary: simplicity, humility, meekness, mortification, and zeal. Simplicity referred not only to leading a simple life without superfluous possessions, but also speaking the truth with absolute candor and transparency and acting with purity of intention—for love of God alone. Humility lies in recognizing our own lowliness and that everything good comes from God. Meekness comprises gentleness, serenity, turning the other cheek to offenses, forgiving the offender, and suppressing anger. Mortification refers to denying pleasures of the senses and subordinating passion to reason. And finally, zeal is the willingness to do anything and go anywhere to evangelize and save souls. These virtues are common themes throughout the writings of St. Vincent de Paul.

> "Every time that some unexpected event befalls us, be it affliction, or be it spiritual or corporal consolation, we should endeavor to receive it with equanimity of spirit, since all comes from the hand of God.'"
> **– St. Vincent de Paul**

St. Vincent de Paul saw an untenable situation in Paris and resolved to do something about it. Several hundred children were being abandoned by their parents every year on the streets of the city. The police routinely took them to a house, La Couche, where they were cared for by a widow and two or three assistants who didn't have the resources to even feed them properly. Many of them soon died, and those who lingered were sedated with narcotics, sometimes fatally. Some were sold, and it was rumored that their blood was used in satanic rituals. The souls of the children taken to La Couche lacked nourishment just as their bodies did. Vincent had some of the ladies who helped him investigate, and when they confirmed the sad plight of these abandoned and orphaned children, Vincent conducted an experiment in 1638 by selecting twelve of them to be cared for in a house by the Sisters of Charity. As donations came in, the number of children grew, and in 1640, Vincent revealed his plan to take charge of all the foundlings of Paris. Executing the plan and sustaining it required a significant fund-raising effort during a time of famine and increasing poverty in France. Eventually, two houses were bought, and King Louis XIV increased the funding initially granted by his mother, the queen dowager. Because of the persistence and determination of St. Vincent de Paul and the commitment of the Sisters of Charity, countless children lived to grow up and know God's love.

"When we receive with an entire and perfect resignation the afflictions which God sends us, they become for us favors and benefits; because conformity to the will of God is a gain far superior to all temporal advantages."
– **St. Vincent de Paul**

When St. Vincent de Paul wrote about the virtue of meekness, he was writing about a virtue he possessed in good measure. When Vincent was serving as the almoner for Queen Marguerite of Valois, he boarded in the same house as an attorney. After a large sum of money was stolen from the attorney, he accused Vincent of having taken it, and he slandered Vincent to everyone he knew. Vincent denied the charge, saying "God knows the truth," and lived under the shadow of suspicion for six years until the real thief confessed. Vincent sometimes told this story to illustrate what meekness looks like, and why patient resignation is the best defense unjust accusations.

"Extend your mercy towards others, so that there can be no one in need whom you meet without helping. For what hope is there for us if God should withdraw His Mercy from us?"
– **St. Vincent de Paul**

Perhaps remembering the two years he spent as a slave in Tunisia after the ship he was aboard was captured by Barbary pirates, St. Vincent de Paul founded a home for former galley slaves. During his time, French convicts were often sentenced to row the Navy's war galleys. It was a brutal existence. Convicts were chained to their benches and stood no chance of surviving if their ship foundered. They were whipped mercilessly to make them row faster or harder until they died or were deemed useless and not worth feeding. Vincent provided a home for them in Marseilles. During the Thirty Years War, Vincent organized relief for those most affected by the hostilities, raising the money he needed to ransom more than 1,200 Christians enslaved in Africa.

> "It is absolutely necessary, both for our advancement and the salvation of others, to follow always and in all things the beautiful light of faith."
> – **St. Vincent de Paul**

In his youth, St. Vincent de Paul was known to be a difficult person to get along with. He described himself as short-tempered and quick to anger and declared that he would still be irascible if it were not for the grace of God. That description doesn't seem to fit the theologian who regarded meekness as one of the five characteristic virtues of a missionary, but those who knew him in his earlier years verified its truth. Through the grace of God and much prayer Vincent increased in humility and became the exact opposite of what he once was—tender, affectionate, sensitive, patient, and infinitely empathetic.

> "Every baptized person should consider that it is in the womb of the Church where he is transformed from a child of Adam to a child of God."
> **– St. Vincent Ferrer**

Legends abound regarding the beginning and end of St. Vincent Ferrer's life. His father had a dream in which a Dominican friar revealed to him that his son would become known worldwide. The story is that Vincent's mother never felt one twinge of pain in giving birth to him. In his later years, St. Vincent preached to St. Colette and her community, and she foretold that he would die in France. He did, in fact, die in Brittany in 1419, at the age of 62. There is disagreement among his early biographers whether Vincent had the gift of tongues because of his ability to convert so many souls on his travels through Europe if he spoke only Valencian.

"Whatever you do, think not of yourself, but of God."
– **St. Vincent Ferrer**

The year before the ordination of St. Vincent Ferrer, the Western Schism tore the Church into two factions. Vincent supported the validity of the Avignon papacy of Clement VII and tried to sway Spaniards to follow him. In 1394, Clement VII was succeeded in the Avignon papacy by Benedict XIII. Though loyal to Benedict XIII and having served him in several positions of increasing importance, Vincent tried (unsuccessfully) to end the schism. Eventually, Vincent withdrew from "combat," asking only to be named apostolic missionary. Some would say that he went on to become the most famous missionary of the 14th century, evangelizing and converting souls throughout Europe, equally welcome in the districts on either side of the schism. He died in 1419, shortly after the schism ended with the election of Pope Martin V.

> "Remember that the Christian life is one of action, not of speech and daydreams. Let there be few words and many deeds, and let them be done well."
> – **St. Vincent Pallotti**

Born in 1795, Vincent Pallotti decided at sixteen to become a priest. He was ordained at the age of 23 and continued on to earn a doctorate in theology and accept a position as assistant professor. He soon found that he preferred pastoral work to academics and spent the rest of his life serving the urban poor. Like St. Philip Neri, to whom he was often compared, Father Vincent established evening classes for general education of the illiterate and unskilled and a number of trade schools in shoemaking, carpentry, horticulture, tailoring, and more. He set up orphanages and homes for girls and established the Society for Catholic Action," to continue his urban mission work and provide services for the poor and underprivileged. Social action was Father Vincent's passion, but it wasn't his only contribution.

> "Since God is perfect in loving man, man must be perfect in loving his neighbor."
> – **St. Vincent Pallotti**

St. Vincent Pallotti is best known for his pioneer work in Catholic social action, but he also envisioned a world in which all souls would belong to Christ. He dreamed of converting all non-Catholics, especially Muslims. There was strong anticlerical sentiment in Rome during the 19th century, accompanied by a decline in public morals. Carnival, intended to mark the beginning of Lent, had become a time of particularly questionable behavior, and Vincent decided to address the situation. During the Roman Carnival of 1825, Father Vincent and an assistant walked through the crowds, their habits a somber note in the atmosphere of gaiety and abandon. They pressed slips of paper into the hands of those they passed, each slip bearing one of these messages: "Life is short, and death comes quickly," "Death strikes even at play," or "One mortal sin merits damnation." Perhaps some of those messages did bring the recipients into the Church, or perhaps not. Either way, this incident is a good example of St. Vincent Pallotti's hands-on approach to doing good in the world.

> "You must be holy in the way that God asks you to be holy. God does not ask you to be a Trappist monk or a hermit. He wills that you sanctify the world in your everyday life."
> – **St. Vincent Pallotti**

During his lifetime, St. Vincent Pallotti was regarded as a mystic and miracle worker, credited with prophecies that came to be realized and several healings. Often, his mere presence was enough for any subsequent healing or cure to be attributed to him. In 1830 or thereabouts, Lucia Fabiani was visited by Father Vincent as she lay dying. He prayed with her to ease her fears and help her trust in God and the Blessed Virgin. Shortly after he left, Lucia told her husband that she was once again healthy. When the doctor arrived to check on her, half expecting her to be dead, his reaction to her obvious cure was, "Don Vincenzo must have been here," though he knew nothing about Father Vincent's earlier visit. On another occasion, Vincent apparently fell into a trance in the confessional and told the penitent that Cardinal Capellari had been elected pope, though no announcement had yet been made by the Vatican and the relatively unknown Capellari's name had not been mentioned among those speculating on the identity of the next pope.

Z

> "A servant is not holy if she is not busy."
> **– St. Zita**

St. Zita is the patron saint of domestic workers for good reason. She was a pious and obedient child who entered domestic service at the age of 12 as the housekeeper for a wealthy weaver and his family eight miles from her home. She was the ideal servant, and she remained with that same family, the Fatinellis, until she died in 1278, at the age of 60. During the 48 years Zita spent with the Fatinelli family, she displayed every virtue one might seek in a servant. She was seen to be extremely devout, charitable, and good-hearted, and over time she went from servant to friend to advisor. Her employers let her set her own work schedule, and she routinely visited the sick and the incarcerated. She is also reported to have had numerous mystical experiences. St. Zita was named saint by popular acclamation upon her death.

Made in the USA
Columbia, SC
01 February 2024